AN INTRODUCTION TO CHRISTIAN WRITING

AN ❖ ETHEL HERR
INTRODUCTION TO
CHRISTIAN
WRITING

For Ruth —
Write on —
and on —
and on

Ethel Herr

1 Cor. 15:58

TYNDALE HOUSE PUBLISHERS, INC., WHEATON, ILLINOIS

All Scripture references are taken from *The Living Bible (TLB)*, the *New American Standard Bible (NASB)*, and the *King James Version* of the Bible *(KJV)*.

Second printing, December 1984
Library of Congress Catalog Card Number 83-50128
ISBN 0-8423-1590-X
Copyright © 1983 by Ethel Herr
Printed in the United States of America

DEDICATION

To
Nina
Barbara
Virginia
Leslee
Alice
Charline
Joyce
Gloria
Janet
Betty
Jane
Bea
Marjorie
Grace Eileen

because you begged me
to help you
answer the question
"Has God called me to write?"

ACKNOWLEDGMENTS

Books do not just happen. They grow, often slowly. From tender roots planted in well-prepared soil long ago, *An Introduction to Christian Writing* sprouted, leafed, budded, and blossomed under the watchful eyes and skillful hands of dozens of literary gardeners. With maternallike care these experts have watered, cultivated, pruned, weeded, trained, and fertilized the growing plant, until at last it is now ready for the decorative basket on the reader's shelf.

Because this is a lifetime-of-learning book, I can never give credit to every gardener to whom credit is due. Many names and faces have vanished from my mind. No reader wants to read the long list a better memory would produce. But a few stand out.

It will never be trite to say that my mother started it all. She aroused in me a love for books and a fascination with the writing process. She praised my childish attempts and endured my atrocious adolescent letters from college. Later, when our family lived in Europe for three years and I wrote a regular family newspaper called *The Holland Herrier,* she looked beyond its imperfections and saw a potential that only a mother could detect. "If you can ever get over being so wordy," she wrote me, "I think you stand a chance of someday becoming a recognized author!"

Neither is it trite to say that without my husband this book never would have come to blossom. He helped me through my studies and encouraged me to develop my abilities. He let me attend conferences and workshops, take on speaking engagements, and teach classes, which gave me something to share and taught me how to share it.

Beyond this, I am grateful to the schoolteachers who taught me good basic skills, put up with my verbose essays, and read my awful stories: to Tricia, my schoolteacher-now-principal friend who gave me my first chance to teach writing skills —to her eighth-grade English students; to the adult education and private writing teachers, the writers and editors from writers' conferences, the authors of writing technique books, and the members of my critique groups who guided and corrected me.

Finally, I will always thank the Lord for those dear women who came to me and begged me to help them answer the crucial question "Has God called us to write?" Their confidence and faithfulness made teaching a reality, a joy, and a source of inspiration. Their successes—and yours as you become effective producing writers—will make the blossoms of this book increasingly bright, profuse, and robust.

CONTENTS

INTRODUCTION

WHAT THIS BOOK CAN DO FOR YOU

So you think you want to write? Perhaps you feel God nudging you toward a typewriter. You have written a few things, perhaps shared them with a friend or even published a poem or an article. Yet, you wonder whether you should be a writer. You wish someone would help you decide and show you how to get started.

You are not alone. Thousands of your Christian brothers and sisters are reading books, taking classes, and attending seminars and conferences on writing and publishing. Their reasons are many.

Some have unusual personal stories to share. Lucille's conversion experience was unique. Gladys worked her way through the trauma of losing a beautiful daughter in an automobile accident. Ron and Linda were used of God in a fruitful pioneer missionary venture. Eileen was delivered by God from a homosexual lifestyle. All these people speak regularly to church groups. If they could write, they could expand their usefulness to a wider audience.

Some already enjoy careers in communications. Howard's pastoral ministry reaches beyond his local congregation to a thriving worldwide tape program. Margaret is a Christian school administrator who shares devotional thoughts with her teachers. Mildred has written poems, skits, and miscellaneous church program materials. Friends, parishioners, and co-workers urge these people to put their ideas into print. But they are preachers, teachers, musicians, and homemakers, not writers. Is this God's voice calling them? Or are they simply hearing suggestions of well-meaning human logic?

Some write in response to an inner compulsion, but have no idea what they are doing. All his life, George has written an assortment of stories, poems, and essays. He has never shown them to anyone, but cannot seem to stop writing. Finally, he has reached a point where he must emerge from his closet and shout to the world. Gloria feels an inner compulsion to bring her idea jottings out of her daily journal and do something useful with them. Fred used to dream of becoming a writer. But the notion was impractical for a family breadwinner. So he wrote little half-completed thoughts, outlines of substantial ideas, bits and pieces, unpolished stories, and pumped gas for a living.

Some must write technical things as a part of their jobs, but feel ill-prepared. Nancy works in a church office, and is responsible for weekly newsletters and bulletins. Jim is an engineer who has to write frequent reports. Do these kinds of writing fall in the category of Christian writing? Can a course in basic Christian writing techniques help them do a better job for the glory of God?

Many aspiring writers are frustrated or confused by circumstances and a lack of know-how. For years Susan has worked on a book. When she finished and presented it to a publisher, she was told to go home and learn to write without preaching. John has also written many things. He frequently sends materials to editors and has even sold a handful of manuscripts. But he has worked entirely on his own and senses large gaps in his learning process. Judy tries to write, but four young children and a busy husband erect formidable barriers to consistency. She would give it up if she could, but something drives her back to the typewriter. How can these people get the counsel they need, learn what is normal in the life of a writer, and find some legitimate shortcuts?

In my years of writing, rubbing shoulders with writers and would-be writers, and teaching beginners, I have met all of these people and more. It seems to me that they are asking one basic question: If God has given me the gift of writing, how shall I go about developing it?

Since you have singled out this book, no doubt you, too, are asking this important question. *An Introduction to Christian Writing* seeks to help you find an answer and to give you the tools needed to get going in the direction that God is leading you.

The outline for this book began to take shape when I prepared to teach my first class of beginning writers. I asked myself, "If I were starting out, what are all the things I now know to be indispensable for effective writing—things I would want someone to teach me before pushing me out into the competitive marketplace?" I jotted down ideas, sorted, rearranged, juggled, expanded, and taught these vital writing starters. Now, I am bringing them together to share with you.

This book has been written with four goals in mind:

1. To emphasize writing as a ministry, an avenue of personal growth, and an act of worship.

2. To teach you how to use the most elementary building blocks of good writing. We will not assume that you already have certain writing skills. We will work on the basics of composition, motivation, and marketing—things every writer needs to know or to review in order to approach writing in a professional manner.

3. To serve as a do-it-yourself manual for learners who may not have a seasoned writer nearby to guide them in their journey through the basics to a writing ministry.

4. To provide a tool for teachers in search of a textbook, supplementary reading, or an outline to use either as is or in adapted form to meet the needs of beginning students.

In order to fulfill these goals, I have divided the book into two sections—the Textbook and the Appendices. The Textbook consists of eleven two-part lessons and a concluding challenge chapter. Part One of each lesson deals with the writer, his person, relationships, attitudes, market study, preparation, and work habits. Part Two gives specific instruction in writing skill areas. It includes examples to help you learn and concludes with detailed assignments for applying materials in the text. You will learn to write, not by simply reading how to do it, but by writing. Hence, the ultimate value of this course depends on your diligent use of these assignments.

By the time you have completed the Textbook section, you will have been introduced to all the major basic skills and theoretical motivational principles needed to launch you as a writer. You will have written at least one manuscript (a narrative account of some personal experience), chosen a market for it, and learned the process for submitting it for publication.

The Appendices contain:

1. A glossary of writers' shop-talk terms.

2. Helps for using this book in a writers' group or class, including some suggested class exercises.

3. Additional writing exercises—outlines of other forms of Christian writing, along with assignments for doing them.

4. Additional information to help you as a writer.

If God has gifted you in the art of writing, there is much that you can do. You will find the instructions in the pages that follow. If writing is not your gift, you will probably make this discovery, as you work your way through these same pages. Proceed prayerfully and diligently, and enjoy your journey into the life, ministry, and labor of a writer.

Lesson One
Part One
What Is a
Christian Writer?

"WRITER" was an elite title I mentally engraved on a gold plaque mounted on a shimmering crystal pedestal. That was before I attended my first writers' conference. I so much wanted to be one of those special people. I was working toward that goal. I had taken three correspondence courses (they seemed less threatening than classes). I had even managed to sell a few *insignificant* bits of my writing—tracts, short short articles, devotionals. All the while, I read writers' conference brochures and dreamed of one day attending one.

Then in 1970 my opportunity came. Mount Hermon Christian Conference Center offered one only thirty miles from home. I was elated at the prospect. With my husband's blessings and checkbook, I paid a ten-dollar deposit, made baby-sitting arrangements with my sister-in-law, and marched off to the fulfillment of my dreams.

Once there, I began to tremble. Standing in the registration line and rubbing shoulders with people I was sure must be real "WRITERS," I felt a dreadful urge to run. What right did I have to be there? Because my husband had paid the fee, I stayed. But I settled one thing from the start. At least I would not discuss any of my work with an editor.

However, one day at lunch I unexpectedly found myself at a table with Joe Bayly, who was not only an accomplished "WRITER" and one of the keynote speakers of the week, but also an important editor from the David C. Cook Publishing Company. I will never know how it happened, but before that meal was over, I had disregarded my resolve and had committed myself to a personal consultation with this awe-inspiring "WRITER," speaker, and *editor*.

Several apprehension-filled hours later, I sat in the shade of a giant Redwood tree with what I decided was the kindest, most human editor alive. He put me so much at ease that I even confessed to him that I was dreaming of attempting a major project.

"I'm afraid it might be too big for me," I admitted. "How can I decide?"

In an incredibly calm and matter-of-fact manner, Joe then offered me the most valuable advice I could have received at that moment, "It's simple," he said. "Just plunge in and attack the thing as if you fully intended to finish it. If you are ready, you will know. If not, you will also know, for you will fall flat on your face."

Eager to find my answer, I went home and charged full speed into my project. Just as Joe Bayly had warned, I promptly fell flat on my face. At that point, my mind, recalling other words of encouragement gained at that same conference, told me that this was not the end. I picked myself up, found a simpler project, and went on. Over the next few years, I finally discovered that with no need for gold plaques, capital letters or a crystal pedestal, I could call myself a writer.

In this book, I want to share Joe Bayly's advice with you, in my own expanded version: *You will never know whether you are gifted in writing until you attack writing as if you had every intention of going all the way.* Do not look back or stop to play with the inevitable doubts. Before you finish these lessons, you will probably have a good idea where you belong. Even if you fall flat on your face with the whole writing process, you will close the book a richer person than you were when you opened it. You will have learned what writing, thinking, and ministering on paper are all about. You will have developed an appreciation for writers and their needs. Above all, you will have become a more effective sharer of your thoughts in every-day relationship situations.

WHAT IS A CHRISTIAN WRITER?

A writer is someone who writes. He may be a *salaried* writer who works on a payroll, performing writing functions for some company or organization. This includes editors, magazine staff writers, public relations specialists, technical writers, and writing teachers.

Perhaps he is a *free-lance professional.* He writes on his own and markets his own work. Very few make a living off their writing in the Christian marketplace. Most free-lancers are part-timers who either hold down another job that puts bread on the table or have a spouse who does.

Many writers are hobby writers, who write principally for the ministry or for the fun of it. Occasionally they sell; more often they do not. These include authors of skits for church programs and poems for birthdays or anniversaries. Most writers do their internship at the hobby level and gradually move on to more ambitious endeavors.

Almost everybody falls in the category of the *everyday writer.* Memos, letters, diaries—we all write something in the routine of daily living.

If you write anything at all, you are a writer. In these lessons, we want to help you improve the quality of your writing so that regardless of how professional you become or do not become, you will do what you do with an expertise that is worthy of the God who has gifted you.

If a writer is a person who writes, *a Christian writer is a writing person who is a Christian.* That is, he/she has a personal relationship with God through Jesus Christ. Many people who are not Christians write for Christian magazines and publishers; they address what they consider to be Christian topics. Selling to the religious market, however, does not turn just anyone into a Christian writer. Most Christian editors are deeply concerned that you, first of all, *be* a Christian if you intend to write for them. Only a Christian by experience can write from a truly godly point of view and meet the needs of growing Christians.

Christians are members of a highly complex body of fellow-believers. Jesus Christ is our Head and gives us our typing orders. For each of us, those orders will be uniquely fitted to our individual capabilities.

Novice writers tend to look at the professionals and say, "Oh, I can't write because I can't do what C. S. Lewis or Marjorie Holmes or John White did. . . ." This is tragic, for while we are excusing ourselves for not being like Eugenia Price, we are missing the opportunities to be ourselves for God on paper and to minister to the audience he has planned for us to serve.

Most important of all, *a Christian writer is a believer at worship*. We tend to think that we are first ministers with a pen. However, before we can minister, we must learn to worship and regard all our writing as an act of worship offered to God. Everything we do and say must be an act of worship, done for God's pleasure. Some of our writing goes on to bless others as well, while some does no more than bless God and ourselves. Whatever else our actions and ministries accomplish, if they do not please him, they have failed.

THE NATURE OF WORSHIP

Worship begins in the heart of the writer. (See John 4:23, 24) It is not basically an outward act performed only in public services. It is a personal, private act of the heart whereby I offer to God my adoration, praise, and thanks for all he is and has done for me, in me, and through me.

Worship reflects the image of God. It shows to me and to my world through me, what God is like. In this way, as I live and write, I am allowing him to live out his personality and his creativity in human form on earth.

Worship also acts in obedience to the revealed will of God. Knowing that to present our bodies a living sacrifice to God is an "intelligent act of worship" (Romans 12:1, *Phillips Modern English)* can help us decide what kinds of things to write. One woman told me that she was considering writing some kind of popular fiction that would sell well. I sensed that she was not comfortable with her decision. When I questioned her, she confessed that she felt this type of thing was actually wrong and that she could not write it with a clear conscience. God never leads us to do what will compromise or violate the established principles revealed in the Bible.

Worship shares openly and honestly what represents our genuine selves. During a casual conversation at my first writers' conference, I heard Professor Carl Johnson say something vital: "We must learn to write out of compression." We know what it is to feel compressed, to be at the point where the whole world is pressing in on us and we wonder whether we can survive. We naturally want to rid our lives of all the tensions that compress us. God does not often honor such a request. He knows that tensions mold us, teach us to cope with life, and give us something to say. If we lived simple carefree lives, how could we command the attention of a world that expects us to show them how to face tension and solve problems?

This advice needs qualification, however. A lot of writers start writing while they are still in the compression chamber. Such writing has value, but only for the writer himself. Recording in your journal your deepest inner feelings at the time of heavy compression is great therapy. However, it is rarely publishable. At the time you write it, it represents such an intense experience you may be convinced that the whole world is just waiting to hear about it.

No, it is not. What it is waiting to hear is what you cannot share until you have reached the "hover level."* This is the "helicopter zone"—neither too high in the clouds to allow you to be in touch with reality, nor so low in the street that your view is limited. Here you are close enough to see what is happening from an objective perspective, without feeling the compression.

Once we have learned to worship on paper, we are free to think about ministering. *A Christian writer is a ministering*

*Also from Mr. Johnson.

prophet with a broken heart. A lot of us like the idea of being prophets. We enjoy scolding people and setting them straight. However, a study of the biblical prophets who preached judgment reveals that they never delivered many words of fire without stopping to weep and plead with the people. "Oh, Israel, if only you would get right with God, you could avoid all this judgment" was a constantly recurring theme. Every recorded prophetic utterance is a show-and-tell exhibit for us as modern prophets with a pen, revealing that rare combination of justice and compassion so typical of God himself. No matter how urgent the message, we must first let God break our hearts with the things that make him weep.

Our writing as a ministry has two functions:

(1) To arrest the attention of a readership that is saturated with ideas and pressures, almost to the point of insensitivity to anything we have to offer. Never before has it been so easy to get the printed word into people's hands. Neither has it been so nearly impossible to get people's honest attention and to penetrate their hearts.

(2) To present all of life from the Christian viewpoint, both to non-Christians and Christians. Our world is dying for the lack of a good, clear image of what God is like. Thousands of people have rejected some erroneous pictures of God that they have seen in a church or in the lives of professing religious persons or in the writings of non-Christians who tried to write about things they did not understand. Few people have rejected the accurately portrayed person of God, for few have had even a fleeting glimpse of him. Providing a clear biblical picture of God is perhaps our greatest challenge.

Finally, in our prophetic ministry, we must recognize that God has called us to be the servants of Jesus Christ and of one another (See Matthew 20:25-28). As servants, we will write to meet others' needs, not our own. We will put ourselves on their level, admit our own weaknesses, and not preach at anyone from some imagined sacred pedestal of arrived learning.

My pastor once gave a profound warning which I repeat to myself often in my writing ministry: "There is always the danger that what begins as a humble service to God will become a desire to be great."[1]

THE WRITER AS CREATOR

If the Christian as a writer is to fulfill God's best with his gift, *he must also be an artist and craftsman.*

When I was a child, I envied anyone who could draw and paint and produce beautiful handicrafts. I was a klutz in the art studio. Everything I tried turned to disaster. To me, the message rang loud and clear—I was no artist. Many years later, I discovered that art was more than painting pictures. I stopped trying to define it and accepted the fact that it was a gift God had given to me, too. The artist in me enabled me to write with form, beauty, and significance. As an artist I could bring pleasure to my reader and to God by including beauty in all I did.

I took a thoughtful look at God the Creator, who is indisputably the Source of beauty and the Master of artistic expression. I noted how important beauty was to him. Many of his greatest treasures of natural beauty are never seen by human eyes. The intricacies of the human body, microscopic flowers and algae tucked away in inaccessible crannies of the earth, trillions of unique snowflake patterns—God gives meticulous care to fashion each of these and more with a precision and beauty we could never imitate. Realizing this, I decided it was not a waste of time to polish the tiny fragments of intimate poetry in my journal, though I might never share them with another human being.

As an artist, I must be careful to inform my readers about man and God and his principles for functioning in this world. By producing good art, I will satisfy both my imagination and that of my readers. Most important of all, I am responsible through my artistic expression to make order out of the chaos of raw life and help my readers do the same.

> Art is ultimately organization. It is searching after order, after form. The primal artistic act was God's creation of the universe out of chaos, shaping the formless into form. . . .[2]

THE WRITER AS CRAFTSMAN

While *art* refers to some mystical innate talent, the *craft* of writing is an exercise in the disciplines of polishing and perfecting our written work. Craftsmanship is workmanship—the 95 percent perspiration that must accompany the 5 percent inspiration before a piece of art can take shape. We will discuss the writer's disciplines in a later lesson. At this point, we need to understand what a craftsman does:

1. *He takes pride in his work.* A craftsman is concerned with quality even more than saleability. Remembering that all we write is an offering of worship to God, dare we consider doing less than our best?

2. *He works with untiring diligence.* Producing simple, readable writing with profound thought content is hard work. The craftsman covets a tribute such as this one given to the Dutch art professor, Hans Rookmaaker: "He had to speak simply, because he thought so deep."[3]

3. *He leaves room for growth in his person and in his writing.* He knows that when living becomes easy, he has nothing to say, and when writing becomes easy, he is not saying it well.

4. *He is able to take criticism and use it constructively in developing his craft.*
   Becoming a Christian writer can best be summarized in Hans Rookmaaker's four steps for producing Christian art.[4] I refer to them frequently as a reminder of the worship and ministry dimensions of my writing. Engrave them on the walls of your mind and heart:
   a. *Weep:* Look around you; see your world. Look within you; know yourself. Look up to God; learn his expectations. Then let him break your heart.
   b. *Pray:* Never rush into publication. Take time to pray each project into being.
   c. *Think:* Do not depend entirely on the tuggings at your heartstrings brought on by weeping. Think your subject through. Research it thoroughly. Produce mature, intellectually sound and honest work.
   d. *Work:* Be prepared to do plenty of this, but never without the other three steps.

Are you called to be a Christian writer? As you learn to weep, pray, think, and work your way through these lessons, examine your heart, sincerely seek God's guidance, and exercise your writing gifts (however small or great they may be). If you do all this, you should begin to find some helpful answers.

Lesson One
Part Two
Perceiving the World

Good writing begins with clear thinking. Clear thinking begins with focused perceiving. All writing consists of original observations of, and reactions to, life. The sharper our skills of observation and perception, the more we will have to say and the better we will be able to say it. Read the parables of Jesus and notice how carefully the Master Communicator observed details and used them in original ways to convey profound messages.

In this section we will discuss three questions: (1) What are the purposes of original perceptivity? (2) How can we increase our perceptivity? (3) How shall we preserve our perceptions?

THE PURPOSES OF ORIGINAL PERCEPTIVITY

1. *It aids the writer in continued personal growth*
   a. By developing alertness and awareness of life,
   b. By preventing boredom and lack of inspiration,
   c. By keeping the life and ministry fresh and current.

2. *It provides materials for the production of lively, readable, practical literature.* Observing your world enables you to

bring new life to anemic sentences. No matter how profound the truth, if you say it in a dull way, your reader will probably turn the page to the next story.

a. Perceptiveness helps you to *show* more than tell.
   Example:

> *Telling:* Lord, if I have to suffer, let me bless other people in the process.

> *Showing:*
> FRAGRANCE
>
> *Lord*
> *If like a fragile flower*
> *Torn petal by petal*
> *My heart must continue to tear*
> *Let there be fragrance.*[5]

b. Perceptiveness helps you to heighten the *emotional tenor* of your writing. Do not tell your reader to laugh or cry. Rather, with perceptive words, paint him a picture so hilarious that he cannot help but laugh or so tender that he feels genuine sorrow and weeps of his own volition.

INCREASING OUR PERCEPTIVITY

1. *Develop an attitude of insatiable curiosity.* Ask, "Why? Where did that come from? How is it done? Where is it going? What if? What made him say that? Why is she the way she is?" People with little curiosity know little beyond the reach of their noses. And what reader cares about such a tight perimeter of facts and opinions?

2. *Try new things.*
   a. Break old patterns. Sit in a different pew in church, drive to a friend's house by a different route, fix something different for breakfast, start with a different section of the newspaper, buy a new kind of outfit, try a new method for baking bread or waxing your car.
   b. Take some risks. Remind yourself that the only sure way

to fail is to refuse to try. Never say, "No," when God says, "Move."

   c. Purposefully broaden your interests. Learn new skills, try new hobbies, eat new foods, visit new places.

3. *Open up your mind.*
   a. To new (or different) types of reading material:
     New magazines, new authors, new styles of writing. Read poetry, science fiction, drama, ancient literature, for example.
   b. To new (or different) ideas:
     Found in new reading material, TV, conversations, music, friends, hobbies, organizations, places. Neither fear new ideas because they are different nor embrace them without thoughtful consideration. Let them stimulate your mind, broaden your areas of concern, and show you new ways of looking at old issues.

     CAUTION: Old ideas are not better just because they are comfortable. Nor are new ideas automatically better just because they appear more relevant to modern society. *Always check new ideas against biblical teachings.* To controversial opinions and viewpoints, avoid the thinking that says:

> *In controversial moments*
>   *my perception's rather fine;*
> *I always see both points of view,*
>   *the one that's wrong and mine.*[6]

Do not fear controversy. If you are confident of God, you can afford to look at all sides of an issue, even those that are obviously erroneous. By careful and prayerful evaluation you will either (1) confirm your present opinion and feel more secure in it, (2) discover the fallacy of your opinion and find truth in some other viewpoint, or (3) come to see that this is an issue which needs more study because there are no simple answers.

     Regardless of your conclusion, you will discover why other people disagree with you. This is vital if you are to communicate compassionately with your readers.

c. To new experiences:
Welcome new experiences and other people's stories of experiences you have never had.

4. *Open your senses.* These are the physical gateways that lead all the impulses from the outside world into our minds and hearts. We must keep them well oiled, active, and in good repair, lest our neglect cause us to miss something important.

SIGHT: Notice the shapes of trees; the shades of color in a rose petal; the sizes of city buildings in relation to one another; the depth dimensions of a living room scene; smiles and how they differ; clothing styles and how they match personalities.... "Today use your eyes as though this day is the only one you will ever see."[7]

TASTE: Do you know how the peas tasted at dinner last night? Do you remember what you had for lunch today? Take time to savor each mouthful. In your mad attempt to gulp down your food in time to meet that next appointment, do not allow all the flavors to blur together.

Sample new food tastes. Note shades and blends of flavors. Find enjoyment at every meal. Do not ignore your tastebuds when you leave the table. How does dust taste beside a roadway? What about ocean spray at the beach? Or nectar from a clover blossom? (What! You've never tried it?)

SMELL: Of course you have smelled bouquets of roses (or have you?). But how about leather, grass, bowls of fruit, summer rain (Is it different from fall rain?), old cedar, a freshly bathed baby, a new car, fabric in a fabric store?

"Follow your nose and let it lead you into new adventures."[8]

HEARING: Never let a dry leaf lie untouched on the sidewalk where you jog or on the street where you ride your bicycle. Dry leaves are for crackling. Listen to a baby's breathing, enjoy a cricket's evening concert or the mockingbird's serenade from a neighbor's TV antenna. Turn off the radio, TV, or stereo, and tune in to the soundful world around you.

TOUCH: A child learns much about his world through touching everything. We mistakenly discard the habit when we become adults. Have you noticed the tremendous variety of textures in your world? Prickliness and smoothness? Hardness and softness? Roughness and silkiness? How do people's handshakes feel different? Do you observe temperatures? Humidity levels? Stuffiness and free-breathing atmospheres?

With a little concentrated practice you can open up your senses and embrace a fascinating world. Once you have formed the habit, you will find yourself slowing down to a reasonable pace, quieting down to a livable volume level, and enjoying life with exhilarating new dimensions.

5. *Open your heart.*
   a. To God's proddings. Spend enough time in Bible study and private prayer to get to know God intimately. This is an essential starting point.
   b. To people. Study people. Do not simply observe that they laugh and cry. Instead, find out what makes them: laugh or cry, bristle or cuddle, be neat and efficient or lazy and sloppy, soothe or lambaste, remember or forget, worship God or ignore him.
   c. To human needs. Not just your own, but those common to all kinds of people. Make lists of the kinds of things that people:

      dream about
      fear
      need
      feel frustrated about
      feel delighted about
      believe in
      sacrifice for.

   d. To emotions and moods. Learn to be sensitive to the prevailing moods in every circumstance in which you find yourself. Record on paper what emotions or moods you feel in surroundings such as:

      a mountain lakeside
      a crowded city street
      a child's hospital room

a family argument
a classroom at exam time
a street on the occasion of a child's first bicycle ride
a room filled with people partying
a cornfield at harvest time.

PRESERVING OUR PERCEPTIONS

Cultivate the notebook habit. Do not trust your memory with all the sensory impressions, new ideas, experiences, and spiritual insights you collect.

FOUR SUGGESTED NOTEBOOKS FOR EVERY WRITER:

1. *Pocket or purse-sized notebook* (two of these). Carry one with you at all times. Keep the other at your bedside. Use it for recording on-the-spot-observations and thoughts. If you are ever stranded without this notebook, use a dinner napkin, a gum wrapper, an envelope—anything you can write on. Keep this notebook up-to-date by later transferring the tidbits you recorded here to their appropriate places in your permanent files for ease of recall.

2. *Personal journal.* A *diary*, which is a record of what *happens* to you every day, may be helpful for your records. BUT a *journal*, which is a record of your *feelings* about or *reactions* to what happens to you each day, is essential. A journal is a *potpourri* of moods, reactions to people and events, sensory perceptions, Bible study notes, prayers—anything that represents how you feel or think. Keeping a journal will do several things for you as a person and will thus make you a more qualified writer:
   a. It will help you work your way through your problems.
   b. It will give you a wealth of material for later writing projects. Just remember that not everything you write in a journal will be valuable to other people.
   c. It will help you grow as a person.
   d. It will give you a place to go back and trace God's goodness in your life.

3. *Idea notebook or file*. This is an organized record of information and ideas; possible article, poem, and story starters; outlines; worksheets; written sources of inspiration for writing.

4. *Quote notebook*. Here you record notes from books you read, sermons you hear, miscellaneous quotes you pick up.

Four suggestions for taking helpful notes:
a. Record material—outlines, quotations, ideas, miscellaneous facts.
b. Jot down ideas suggested by what you read, hear, and/or observe.
c. Record your personal reactions to, and questions arising from, what you read or hear.
d. Always include details of the source of your notation. Remember to put quotation marks around all the direct quotes you copy.

ASSIGNMENT

1. Obtain the four notebooks suggested in this lesson and begin to use them.
   a. Purse or pocket-sized notebooks (two).
   b. Daily journal. Dated diary book is best for beginners, as it encourages you to write something every day.
   c. Loose-leaf binder or set of file folders for idea file or notebook. You may use the Idea File Worksheet as an outline for setting up your idea file or notebook on pages 31, 32.
   d. Loose-leaf binder or stenographer's pad for copying important quotes.
2. Each day of the next week, jot down all the observations you can make, using the following plan:
   Day 1—Sight observations
   Day 2—Taste observations
   Day 3—Smell observations
   Day 4—Hearing observations
   Day 5—Touch observations
   Day 6—Mood observations
   Day 7—Idea observations

3. Choose a mood or an action photo from a magazine or a newspaper. What mood does it portray? Record all the sensory impressions and ideas the picture either shows or suggests to you. You may either list your observations or write an essay or story incorporating them.

[1] Paul Steele, pastor of The Valley Church, Cupertino CA.

[2] Laurence Perrine, *Sound and Sense* (New York: Harcourt, Brace and World, 1956), p. 183.

[3] Lynette Martin, *Hans Rookmaaker* (Downers Grove IL: InterVarsity Press, 1979), p. 105.

[4] Hans Rookmaaker, *Art Needs No Justification* (Downers Grove IL: InterVarsity Press, 1979), pp. 23—25.

[5] Ruth Harms Calkin, *Tell Me Again, Lord, I Forget* (Elgin IL: David C. Cook Publishing Co., 1974), p. 19.

[6] Source unknown.

[7] Edna Kaehele, *Sealed Orders* (Englewood Cliffs NJ: Prentice-Hall, 1959), p. 14.

[8] Ibid., p. 16.

IDEA FILE WORKSHEET

SECTION I—WHO AM I?
1. Autobiographical sketch (brief summary of your life history and future projections)
2. Family (facts about immediate family and ancestral roots)
3. Places I've lived or visited
4. Skills I have acquired
5. Hobbies I enjoy
6. Interesting people I have met
7. Ministries I have been involved in
8. Significant experiences I have had
9. My strong points
10. My limitations and weaknesses
11. My feelings about important issues
12. My personal philosophy
13. My church
14. My community

SECTION II—SUBJECTS I WOULD LIKE TO LEARN MORE ABOUT

SECTION III—THINGS I AM LEARNING
1. Words and phrases
2. Pictures
3. Sensory observations
4. People
5. Songs
6. Jokes
7. Interesting experiences of other people
8. Unusual things I observe
9. Problem situations
10. Thought-provoking ideas
11. Philosophies
12. Viewpoints on important issues

SECTION IV—SUBJECTS TO WRITE ABOUT
1. Article ideas
2. Personal experiences
3. Themes

4. Problems and plots
5. Devotional ideas
6. Others

SECTION V—IDEA STARTERS
(Newspaper clippings, articles, idea germs, anecdotes—anything that might trigger an idea. See Lesson 5 for more ideas.)

SECTION VI—OUTLINES AND WORKSHEETS
(Learn more about these in future lessons.)

Lesson Two
Part One
What Are the Christian Writer's Opportunities?

Suppose an epidemic is sweeping through your community, killing thousands of helpless victims. Doctors, in their antiseptic professional office suites, are wringing their hands as they watch patients (and each other) succumb, despite frantic efforts to prescribe powerful antidotes. In your hand, you hold a special drug that will certainly cure your dying neighbors. You know. It has cured you and your friends of the same disease.

What action will you take?

"I'll get out where the sick people are and dispense the life-saving medicine," you say. "That is only logical."

Do you not know that you will get some resistance and lots of skepticism?

"True enough," you respond. But you know it works. So you are willing to take the chance of being rejected by the doubters and to share your cure with all who will accept it.

Whether you realize it or not, you live in a community that is dying from an epidemic. It is called *sin*. If you are a Christian, you also hold the only life-giving formula available which will both cure that disease and restore a strong, vibrant, healthy life. Further, you are constantly learning new secrets to help both you and your neighbors to grow stronger and more resistant to relapses and anemic spells.

34

What action will you take?

No doubt you are already deeply involved with a number of effective methods for sharing the divine cure for the ultimate human malady. Yet you know that if God has called you to a writing ministry, nothing will fit your unique capabilities and insights like spreading the message via the printed page.

Often, however, as you sit at your typewriter, discarding rough draft sheets; hassling with outlines, plots and images; trying to coax obstreperous words and sentences into smooth cooperation, you will hardly be overwhelmed with a great sense of accomplishing any divine mission so noble as "rescuing the perishing." Those are the moments when you will need to remind yourself that "as Christian authors, we are mediators between God's help and man's hurt."[1]

In order to clarify the vision of your gift, it helps to get practical—ask a few questions and survey the possible answers. Shall you write fiction short stories for Sunday school papers? Poems for literary magazines? News stories and PR releases for our churches? How-to books? Devotional articles? Scholarly apologetics for the Christian faith? Where is the niche that God has carved out just for you?

In this lesson, I want to begin by giving you a quick overview of the types of opportunities (or markets) and the variety of literary forms from which you can choose. Then I will give you four simple guidelines for choosing the kinds of markets suitable to your writing gift. Finally we will consider a dozen solid rewards for answering God's call to write.

In today's society, we have at least three channels for expressing ourselves and delivering our messages. *First is the medium of the printed page*, the one with which you will most likely be working. In fact, it forms a basis for all mass communications. *Second are the audial media*—tapes, radio, speeches, music, any forum where people receive messages by listening with their ears. *Third are the visual media*, including photography and the dramatic arts, both onstage and in movies and TV. These are often combined with the audial.

Most audial and visual media depend on the printed page in one way or another. Cassettes and radio productions begin with someone's ideas being scripted for the producer to work with. Plays and movies rely on scripts as well. Many speeches are written out and read verbatim. Multi-media productions each use photography, music, and scripts all focused around a central theme, which is first written down.

Writing markets fall into two general categories: broad and specific.

BROAD CATEGORIES

1. *Secular and Christian markets.* The Christian market is more accessible to us. In some ways it is easier to "crack." It allows us to share our ideas in terms that we feel comfortable with. However, we can make a tremendous impact on the world by writing for the secular market. The world needs to be exposed to God's point of view. Who but a Christian is capable of doing the job?

2. *Fiction and nonfiction markets.* The Christian fiction market is highly limited. A lot of Sunday school papers take short stories. A much wider market exists in the secular press. If you can learn to write well, this may be a highly effective avenue for your fiction talent.

   Fiction is a valid genre, a valuable tool for presenting organized truth to persons who are not yet ready or willing to face it in the more direct sermonic (didactic) forms of nonfiction. Jesus taught us this by his frequent use of parables.

3. *Limited circulation and general markets.* Limited circulation markets include consumer, technical, literary, and house organ types of magazines. These are highly specialized in their appeal and readership. General markets reach the general public and have a wide appeal to all kinds of readers.

SPECIFIC CATEGORIES

1. *Books* of all kinds—nonfiction books, novels, resource books, gift books, children's books, technical books, and booklets.

2. *Magazines.* These are further divided into many types—family magazines, women's magazines, sports magazines, and the like.

   In the religious market, we need to be aware of five important kinds of magazines:

   a. General (e.g., *Moody Monthly, Decision, Eternity)*
   b. Denominational (e.g., *Evangelical Beacon, Lutheran Digest, The Mennonite)*
   c. Thematic or Special (e.g., *Family Life Today* for families; *Success* for Christian educators; *Christianity Today* for pastors; *Virtue* for women; *His* for college students; *The Christian Reader,* a digest of Christian magazines)
   d. Organizational house organs (e.g., *Africa Now* from Sudan Interior Mission; *World Vision* from World Vision; *In Other Words* from Wycliffe Bible Translators)
   e. Age categories (e.g., *Young Teen Power, Primary Days, Campus Life)*

3. *Miscellaneous markets.* Editorial offices need writers of various sorts. Organizations need PR people to plan publicity programs and write news releases, brochures, and newsletters. They also need writers of organizational histories. Many churches produce these histories for special anniversaries. Schools need teachers of writing technique, literature, and speech. Radio and TV networks and producers of educational materials hire writers. In today's shrinking world, where such a high priority is being placed on communication skills, writers are needed in a large number of places and situations.

   Not only is the marketplace wide and varied, but the literary forms you can choose from in fashioning your thoughts are also many—limited largely by your imagination and creativity.

   Perhaps you dream of writing a *book*, either fiction or nonfiction. This is probably an unrealistic place to begin. Instead you would do better to learn your craft on smaller projects. Try the magazines with your *articles, short stories, poems, essays, puzzles, letters,* and *short filler items* (anecdotes, jokes, interesting but little-known facts, epigrams, lists of ideas).

Photo essays are a fascinating combination of pictures with a brief text, producing a choice work of art that usually informs and always inspires. Other kinds of writing include *plays, skits, radio and TV scripts, news stories, book reviews, newsletters, brochures, instructions, ghost writing* (writing someone else's story), and *co-authoring.* (These last two projects can be difficult; do not start here, especially with a friend you want to keep.)

With so many markets and forms from which to choose, how can you possibly decide where to begin? In Part 1 of Lessons 7 (choosing markets) and 8 (choosing forms), we will go into this in detail and give some tools for evaluating and analyzing the markets you consider. At this point, we want to encourage you to begin observing the market and the forms. If you are not a book or a magazine worm, become one. Pick up and examine every magazine you can find.

Use spare minutes in a doctor's office, for example, to browse through magazines. Spend an occasional day in the periodical section of your public or church library studying magazines with which you are not familiar. Ask friends for copies of magazines they no longer want. Study magazine racks in local stores. Check with your church librarian or the library of any Bible colleges that may be located near you. Other churches in your area will, no doubt, have copies of their denominational magazines that you can examine.

As you look at these many magazines with an eye for where you would like to submit what you write, keep these four things in mind:

1. Try for the markets that you enjoy, admire, and feel comfortable with as a reader.

2. Try for markets within your reach. If you have a tough skin, aim for the top. If you start at the bottom, you will never know how far you can go. But when the rejections come in from the top, do not stop. Move on down the line.

3. Do not despise the small markets. Plan to write as well as you can, regardless of the magazine you aim for. Remember that if God is in your venture, he alone knows how large or prestigious a market is just right for your literary

work and your developing character. Trust him, swallow your pride, and start wherever you need to start.

"Good work cannot be done while you have your tongue in your cheek and are looking down your nose,"[2] says Phyllis Whitney.

4. Get acquainted with a wide variety of markets in different categories that appeal to you. We have already suggested ways by which you can get an initial exposure to many magazines. One thing I like to do in order to keep abreast of the continuing progress and changes taking place in the market is to subscribe to a different magazine every year. One year it is *Christian Herald;* another it is *Lutheran Digest;* another, I choose *Guideposts* or *Alive Now.* Often my choices reflect certain areas of interest I am researching for a subject I want to address later on.

In the beginning, take a market listing of some sort and find five magazines for which you think you would like to write. Then, write letters to each of these markets, requesting a sample copy of their magazine along with editorial guidelines for writers. (See Assignment 1 at the end of Part 2 of this lesson for specific instructions.)

With the sin epidemic raging all around you as you struggle to dispense God's Word through your consecrated typewriter, you may be blessed to see *persons transformed by the power of God through what you have written.* Indeed, this is the highest goal of a writing ministry/career and the source of the greatest possible satisfaction.

At the same time, God is gracious to give you a harvest of other rewards as well:

1. Writing will give you a vocation that allows you to work in your own home, to set your own schedule, and to work on your own.

2. It satisfies some tremendous God-given creative urges.

3. It provides you the satisfaction of seeing your work in print.

4. It helps you as a co-worker with God to develop a genuine wholesome pride in your workmanship.

5. It may bring you some financial rewards.

6. It opens many doors and windows of learning on your world.

7. It expands your world by putting you in touch with fascinating people and providing you with priceless friendships.

8. It broadens your ministry, allowing your life to touch an increasingly wide radius of other lives.

9. It opens doors on new kinds of ministry.

10. It aids in your own personal growth.

As you the writer struggle with the challenges, priorities, and discouragements of your writing gift, it will develop and refine in you at least eight special characteristics:

1. an ability to scrutinize
2. the excitement of discovery
3. a capacity for analyzing and evaluating
4. a heightened curiosity
5. mental alertness
6. flexibility and patience
7. powers of empathy
8. deep appreciation for God.

Several years after my first writers' conference, I met Joe Bayly again, this time at a Sunday school convention. He asked about my writing. I was bubbling with excitement about all the opportunities God had led me to tackle since that memorable afternoon when Joe had first encouraged me to start acting like a writer. With enthusiasm, I told him, "It's been a wonderful adventure. I now know that God has called me to write and I love it. Isn't that amazing?"

He smiled and, in his characteristic fatherly manner, shared his own experience with discovered identity: "I understand. It was a great day for me when I, too, learned that God was pleased to let me do the thing I most enjoyed doing."

When you have exercised your skills and stretched yourself to grasp a host of new and sometimes frightening opportunities, you, too, may one day make the thrilling discovery that you love to write because God has called you to be a writer. The key lies in what you do with the opportunities he gives you along the way.

Lesson Two
Part Two
Choosing Appropriate Words

Good writing begins with clear thinking. In Lesson 1 (Part 2) we noted that this takes place only when we observe and perceive our world in all its shapes and colors, sounds, tastes, smells, and moods. As you opened your senses and emotions, you recorded what you discovered. The tools you used as an essential link between ideas perceived and ideas shared were WORDS.

The process is illustrated by this diagram:

PHASE ONE

Step 1: The senses and the mind *perceive* an idea or the glimmer of an idea.
Step 2: The imagination *preserves* and *shapes* the idea.
Step 3: The pen *concretizes* it in WORDS.

PHASE TWO

Step 1: The senses and the mind *read* the WORDS.
Step 2: The imagination *re-creates* and *evaluates* the writer's idea.
Step 3: The whole person *responds* in lifestyle.
Step 4: The mouth or the pen *shares* the idea with others, in WORDS.

WORDS AND IDEAS

Good writers have an incurable love affair with words. One of my favorite poems shares the contagion of such a writer's enthusiasm in genuine show-and-tell method:

I LIKE WORDS

by Margaret Caskey

I like words—
Silvery words that tinkle
Across the page like delicate wind chimes;
Like the full-throated shouting of strong men;
Solemn words that bring a catch to my throat
Like kneeling before an altar.
I like pompous, frock-coated words
That puff out their waist-coats like fat politicians
Strutting importantly across the page;
Eager, impetuous words that come racing and tumbling over
    each other
To reach the end of the sentence;
Comfortable words that purr contently
Like a cat upon the hearth.
I like crisp, scintillant words
Like the flashing cut of a knife;
Artless, carefree words that sing like happy children;
Friendly, folksy words still with the look of homespun on
    them;
Words that can make a living, breathing thing
Out of a scrap of rag and pulp,
That can make an impassioned oration out of empty air.
I like words. The empty white of paper
Catches at my pen in an insistent plea to be peopled.
I like words.[3]

In order to help you develop this same sort of love for, and expertise in, handling words and understanding their roles, let us look at (1) the functions of words, (2) some guidelines for choosing effective words, and (3) suggestions for increasing your arsenal of words.

THE FUNCTIONS OF WORDS

1. *Words influence people and cause them to:*
   a. Think or to change their minds
   b. Feel strong emotions
   c. Develop character and attitudes
   d. Take action
   e. Share their own thoughts with others.
   Someone has said that "words rule the world."[4]

2. *Words symbolize ideas:* Words are the embodiment of those concepts that our minds are constantly acquiring and refining and that our social natures urge us to share with others. If we choose our words poorly, we defeat communication. Hence, proper choices are critical.

3. *Properly chosen words make our writing:*
   a. *Clear,* so that the reader need never guess what we mean.
   b. *Accurate,* so that the reader can trust our credibility.
   c. *Vivid,* so that the reader can enjoy our work and enter into the experience we share or share the conclusions we have reached.

CHOOSING EFFECTIVE WORDS

1. *Use clear and simple words.* Do not let your love affair with words carry you away and short-circuit clarity and readability.
   Example:

   > *Bad:* I am experiencing a discomforting biliousness in the area of my abdomen.
   > *Better:* I feel sick at my stomach.

   WHAT TO AVOID:
   a. *Flowery words:* overly elegant, high-flown, affected words that overdo the emotional impact. They are superficial and artificial, and say little of worth.

Examples:

> our noble heritage
> dear old Dad

b. *Sentimental words:* emotional, gushy, tear-jerking words without any substance. " ... indulgence in emotion for its own sake.... It revels in old oaken buckets, rocking chairs, mother love, and the pitter-patter of little feet; it oversimplifies; it is unfaithful to the full complexity of human experience."[5]

c. *Preachy words and phrases:* primarily moralizing, usually dull, trite, and flat words.
Examples:

> as you can see, now, friend, tell me, repent, obviously

d. *Unnecessary words:* repetitious words, words that do nothing to further the action, clarify ideas, or create moods and settings.
Example:

> *Poor:* The family in *this modern-day* twentieth century has come *very much* closer to *a real* extinction than at any other time in the entire history *of the world.*
>
> *Improved:* The family in the twentieth century has come closer to extinction than at any other time in history.

My mother once taught me: "Never use the word *very,* unless it is very, very, very important." The same advice is also good for the following words and phrases:

almost	oh
actually	well
practically	probably
naturally	obviously
virtually	tiny
suddenly	it goes without saying
really	as you can see
absolutely	undoubtedly

as you must know   anyway
so   then
but   positively
just   definitely
little

Words should be chosen because they best express the writer's meaning, not because they display the writer's impressive vocabulary.[6]

2. *Use strong, active, direct words.* Rely mostly on nouns and verbs; use adverbs and adjectives sparingly. Think of nouns as the skeletons that provide structure and stability for your sentences. Picture your verbs as the sinews and muscles that give strength and make action possible.

   a. Replace adverb-verb combinations with picturesque, active verbs.
      Example:

      Weak: He *wrote sloppily* on the page.
      Better: He *scrawled* across the page.

   b. Replace adjective-noun combinations with picturesque, specific nouns.
      Example:

      Weak: She laid her baby in the *tiny infant-sized bed with rockers.*
      Better: She laid her baby in the *cradle.*

   c. Replace forms of the verb *to be* with active verbs that do something.
      Example:

      Weak: He *was eating* his dinner hastily.
      Better: He *bolted down* his dinner.

   Interrogate every adverb (most of which end in *ly)* and every *to be* word; make it give you three good reasons why it should be allowed to live.

   d. Say things in a direct way.
      Example:

46

> *Bad:* A great time was had by all.
> *Better:* Everyone had a great time.

Note how strong, active words make the following two examples more vivid and enjoyable.

> *Weak:* Giant sheep *are spread abroad* in their high pasture *in great numbers.*
> *Strong:* "The giant sheep *tumble and frisk about* in their high pasture, until the world *tires of counting them.*"[7]

> *Weak:* The onions *were the size* of hamburgers.
> *Strong:* "Sweet onions *swelled out to the circumference* of a hamburger."[8]

   e. Unless essential to convey accurate meanings or for emphasis, avoid opening sentences with conjunctions such as *and, but, so, then, for,* and *also.*

3. *Use precise words.* Often only one word exists that will communicate your meaning clearly, accurately, vividly. In poetry this is particularly true. Because it is such a concentrated form of thought, every word has to be perfect.
   a. *Accurate words.* When in doubt, check your dictionary for both definitions and correct usage. Often two words are almost synonymous. But there is a slight shade of difference in meaning. Becoming a master of these trifles helps to mark you as a skilled craftsman.
   b. *Specific words.* Since you want to be vivid, avoid general words wherever possible.
   Example:

> *Weak:* flowers
> *Specific:* pansies, petunias, violets

4. *Use show-and-tell words.*
   a. *Words that paint pictures.*
   Example:

> "Kerosene lamps flickered, their soft glow making amber ovals on the ceiling."[9]

"his disheveled hair and unruly beard blowing easily with the occasional breeze, as though he were brother to the wind."[10]

"fire flutters in gentle waves."[11]

Picture words are also called "imagery," and fall into two categories:

Metaphors: Figures of speech that imply a similarity between unlike things, without stating it directly.
Example:

"He clasps the crag with crooked hands."[12]

Similes: Figures of speech that directly express a similarity between unlike things.
Example:

"And like a thunderbolt he falls."[13]

b. *Words that make sounds.*

These fall into three categories:

Assonance: Duplication of internal vowel sounds.
Examples: fr*ee* and *ea*sy, sl*a*pd*a*sh, h*o*ld-s*oa*k
Alliteration: Duplication of initial sounds.
Examples: *t*wisted *t*wine of *t*ime, *f*ish and *f*owl
Onomatopoeia: Words that sound like their meaning.
Examples: clinking, poof, roar, rumble, clash

c. *Words that create moods.*

1) Through the inner sound and rhythm of the words themselves.
Example:

Keeping time, time, time
In a runic sort of rhyme,
To the tintinnabulation that so musically wells
From the bells, bells, bells, bells, bells, bells . . .
Hear the loud alarum bells—
Brazen bells!
What a tale of terror, now, their turbulency tells![14]

2) Through the images evoked by the words.
Example:

> Ball of kitten fluff
> Curled to sleep in childish arms
> Warmth snuggles to warmth.

In the following two poems, notice the difference in the way words create moods. One poem uses words that *tell us of the mood.* Underline these words as you read the poem. The other poem paints a picture of a scene that *shows us the mood.* Which of the two does a more effective job of creating the mood?

A FROZEN WINTER DAY

A frozen winter day when all is still
  Is a sad and lonely thing;
The ice and cold to the sensitive soul
  Do melancholy bring.

No sound is on the heavy winter air,
  No birds their chantings start,
And there is nothing but despair.
  Within the empty heart.[15]

A WIDOW BIRD SATE MOURNING

A widow bird sate mourning for her love
  Upon a wintry bough;
The frozen wind crept on above,
  The freezing stream below.

There was no leaf upon the forest bare,
  No flower upon the ground,
And little motion in the air
  Except the mill-wheel's sound.[16]

5. *Use original words and phrases.* Overused ways of saying things are called "clichés." They lull the reader to sleep or invite him to pick another book or story. Clichés are words or phrases once bright with color, full of activity and mood (e.g., rough as sandpaper, quick as a wink, smooth as butter, a burden for souls). Through much use and familiarity, they have become scuffed, dull, and unimaginative, lacking the

power to evoke the vivid images they were created to evoke.

Sidney Cox calls clichés "overdomesticated symbols . . . for short cuts . . . Like shells that once sheltered and grew with living creatures, but they are empty now and crushed to build highways. They suffice for uneventful transportation."[17] Most of our comfortable Christian language is a form of clichés or specialized jargon. Learn to write about being born again without using the term "born again." While there is a place to use it, we should most often replace it with some phrase that will have meaning for the reader who has never read John 3.

Avoid the unnecessary repetition of words. This can create a dull, first-grade-readerish style. Often the use of a synonym or a change in sentence arrangement adds variety to your writing or conveys your meaning more accurately.

However, repetition may be valuable to communicate your precise meaning, to preserve a free and natural style, or for emphasis.

How to find the balance between dull repetition and affected originality? Do not repeat words excessively when there is a better way to say what you want to say. But do not use synonyms just for the sake of avoiding repetitions. Synonyms must be functional.

Example of avoiding repetition:

> *Bad:* The dog ate all of *the dog's* dinner.
> *Better:* The dog ate all of *his* dinner.

Example of using repetition:

> *Awkward:* She chose a bright red book from the *shelf of bound volumes.*
> *Better:* She chose a bright red book from the *bookshelf.*

INCREASING OUR ARSENAL OF WORDS

1. Polish the art of alert observation and thoughtful interpretation. (See Lesson 1, Part 2.)
2. Read widely. Read a variety of authors, styles, literary forms, subjects. Read the *Reader's Digest* section, "Toward More Picturesque Speech." Read quality literature and colorful writing.

50

3. Get a dictionary and use it. Check it for spellings, pronunciations, definitions, usage, synonyms, word origins. A good dictionary will help you to know when to use which synonym for a specific purpose. Usage dictionaries and synonym finders or a thesaurus are also helpful.

   If in doubt, look it up. Better right than shoddy, especially when your manuscript sits in an editor's balance scales.
4. Begin to make lists of words. Add these to your idea notebook. List new words or words that strike you as being particularly effective as you read or listen to conversations. Make lists of colorful words, active words, precise words, mood words, sensory words, rewritten clichés.
5. Write poetry. This is the best exercise I know of for learning how to use words to the best advantage. In poetry, every word has to be just right—right meaning, right tone, right color, right mood, right rhythm. The smaller the poem, the more this is true. Learning to write good poetry cannot help but improve the quality of your prose.

ASSIGNMENT

1. Go to your public library and check out the most recent December issue of *The Writer* magazine. Toward the back, you will find a lengthy list of religious markets with guidelines. Look through the list and pick five markets that you think you might like to write for. Using the sample letter below (or one of your own composition—keep it short!), write to each of the five target markets requesting editorial guidelines and sample copies. Enclose one dollar with each request, unless more is indicated.

SAMPLE LETTER

Your name and address
Date

Name of Editor (if given in guidelines)
Name and address of magazine
Dear—(use name of editor given in the guide):

Please send me a sample copy of your magazine, along with any editorial guidelines you wish to share with freelance writers. Thank you.

Sincerely,

As you receive replies from these markets, make a file card for each market (See example below). File these alphabetically. Later, as you submit materials to the markets, we will show you how to record submission information on the cards as well.

SAMPLE FILE CARD

DECISION, 1300 Harmon Place, Minneapolis MN 55403
George Wilson, Managing Editor

2. In your idea notebook make lists of new words, effectively used words, simple words, active words, colorful words, specific words, mood words, rewritten clichés, sensory words, idea words.
3. Do the following assignment sheet on words.

[1] Anne Harrington, "Actualize Your Potential," *Successful Writers' and Editors' Guidebook* (Carol Stream IL: Creation House, 1977), p. 39.

[2] Phyllis Whitney, *Writing Juvenile Fiction* (Cincinnati: The Writer, 1947), p. 34.

[3] Margaret Caskey, "I Like Words." By permission. From the 1942 issue of *Word Study* © 1942 by Merriam Webster, Inc., publishers of the Merriam Webster ® Dictionaries.

[4] According to the *Famous Writers Course,* Vol. 1, p. 99, this came from "a great jurist in the 17th century."

[5] Perrine, *Sound and Sense*, p. 201.

[6] Earle Cairns, *God and Man in Time* (Grand Rapids MI: Baker Book House, 1978), p. 163.

[7] Alan H. Olmstead, *In Praise of Seasons* (New York: Harper & Row Publishers, Inc., 1977), p. 11.

[8]Ibid., p. 19.

[9]Duane Phelps, "The Simple Life," *Family Life Today,* November 1979, p. 25.

[10]William H. Stephens, *The Mantle* (Wheaton IL: Tyndale House Publishers, Inc., 1976), p. 168.

[11]Ibid., p. 199.

[12]Alfred Lord Tennyson, "The Eagle."

[13]Ibid.

[14]Edgar Allan Poe, "The Bells."

[15]Perrine, *Sound and Sense*, p. 214.

[16]Ibid.

[17]Sidney Cox, *Indirections* (New York: Alfred A. Knopf, 1947), p. 34.

WORDS WORKSHEET _____

1. Rewrite the following sentences, simply (rather than complexly) using strong verbs and direct statements.

   She *spoke hastily.*
   The weather *looks bad.*
   The old man *is sitting quietly* on the bench.
   A picnic lunch *was brought by* each child.
   The line was *hit by* the fullback.

2. Change the following general words into specific words:

   tree
   shoe
   music
   home
   storm
   building
   stand
   eat

3. Rewrite each of these clichés, using the kinds of words discussed in this lesson.

   white as snow
   as luck would have it
   the things of the Lord
   salvation
   spiritual blessing
   those pearly gates
   incarnation
   power of God

Lesson Three
Part One
Am I Qualified to Be a Christian Writer?

You are a writer of some sort, even if you never write anything more than occasional notes to your family and post them on a bulletin board. But do you have what it takes to become more than an everyday writer?

In order to help you decide, let's start at the top. What are the qualifications for becoming a constantly producing writer —a pro or a semipro?

As you start through the list, you may be tempted to close the book and run off to some other more worthwhile activity. But wait. Resist that urge. So you do not think you have all the characteristics you need? Very likely you possess more than you realize. You have simply not developed them well enough so that you recognize or feel assured of them. As long as you have an irresistible urge to write and God keeps nudging you toward the typewriter, there is hope. Just go to work on the weak areas, and the potential you uncover will amaze you.

Determination is the key.

I saw this sort of determination in a young man I knew. He was a sophomore in high school when he announced to his family: "I am going to become a lawyer." His parents looked at his academic record and skill levels and reminded him, "A lawyer must have top-notch writing skills, and that is one of your weakest areas."

The boy was undaunted. "I've made up my mind to be a lawyer. I can learn to write!"

That is the winning kind of attitude that will carry you through to the highest level of professionalism in your writing. Keep it always clearly before you as you consider the things you need to put you in the producing/selling category.

1. *Besides determination, we need a love for God and a desire to see him honored.* This should go without saying, but when it does, we tend to forget it. It is impossible to be truly Christian writers unless we are committed above all else to putting his desires, his plans, his standards first. Is our number-one goal to please him in all we do, say, think, write? If not, we have some work to do in our own hearts before we are ready to write.

   One student wrote, "I was a dutiful servant, but God wanted a daughter." A dutiful servant may serve solely for pay, while hating his master at each step. The daughter serves out of a strong loyalty born of love.

2. *We need a love for people and a desire to serve them at their point of need.* Loveless preachers (in the pulpit or at the typewriter) are what Paul calls "noisy gongs" (1 Corinthians 13:1, Williams). That is quite a contrast to the Spirit-filled communicators God calls us to be. We cannot love people unless we are willing to listen to them. Creative people often feel that they must do all the talking. If we never learn to shut our mouths and open our ears and hearts, we will have no way of knowing what our brothers and sisters need. Listening gives us a clear vision of what needs to be said and a gentle way to say it.

3. *We need personal spiritual depth and vision.* Always skimming along the top of life, a shallow person takes one day at a time without asking, "Why?" or "Where does this come from?" or "Where will this lead me?" He never bothers to think things through. Such an individual has nothing to offer to others. Someone has said we should never be satisfied to be the immature persons we are today. No matter how mature we are today, we still have a long way to go.

Our goal as Christian writers is indeed to help change our world, but we cannot begin until we have allowed God to change us.

4. *We need a consistent Bible study and prayer life.* You say, "But I don't intend to write Bible study materials." That makes no difference. Diligence in Bible study and prayer will help make us into the whole persons God can use to communicate his truth to a world of fractured persons.

   A consistent devotional life will also give us a strong biblical perspective on all we write, as well as an intimacy with God that will assure us of guidance in making our writing his ministry rather than our successful ego trip. Russ Chandler, religion writer for the *Los Angeles Times,* once said, "Relate the Bible to the inner circle of modern issues and problems." This is not easy. We cannot expect to solve all of the world's thorny issues in our writing. The Bible simply does not have pat answers for every problem of society. Because many issues are complex and take years of working through, we should not expect to solve them all in a series of smooth three-point articles for *Time* magazine. The fact that we cannot find simple solutions does not relieve us of the responsibility to search out answers in the Bible. God calls us to dedicate our lives to this process.

5. *We need enthusiasm.* Are you excited about your writing? About what you have to say? About Jesus Christ? Are you excited that you have life and breath? That God has given us trees in dozens of shapes and sizes and shades of green? Are you enthusiastic over all that life has to offer? If you live in the doldrums, do not wonder if editors never sit up and take notice. Certainly no reader will give your writing more than a ho-hum glance and hurried brush-off.

   Ask God to give you an enthusiastic, positive attitude toward life. Then ask him to give you ideas and burdens that you can really care about sharing with others.

6. *We need the ability to discern significance.* You are working to increase your awareness of your world and its ideas; you

58

are broadening your horizons. You are learning to pick up an inexhaustible array of experiences and observations. Are they all fuel for your writing?

No. Dozens of them are the elemental trivia of which life is composed. You need them to add substance and color to your life. You jot them in your journal or idea notebook so you will understand them better. A few of them will find their way into a manuscript here or there. The bulk will not leave the seclusion of your files.

If your writing is to be on target and meet needs, you need to learn which of the fascinating and dramatic happenings that befall you are of consequence to other people and which are nothing more than grist for the learning mill and inspirational reading in your private journal. Regardless of how significant a thing looks to you, examine it carefully and ask, "Will anybody else care about this? Will the lives of others be enriched by reading about it? Will it help them to cope with similar problems?"

Isolating the true significance of events is costly in the life of the writer. We learn life-changing truth only through the process of suffering and grappling with difficult problems. When God sends a problem, a trial, or a prolonged pressure point into your life, the natural reaction is to pray, "Lord, get me out of this!" Most likely, his response will be, "Let me take you through it." This is the only way we can learn to find solutions *worth sharing* with a hurting world. In the words of a small quotation that hangs above my desk: "True creativity comes not from the removal of tension, but from the acceptance of it."[1]

7. *We need the courage to speak up, even when our message may be unpopular.* There are times when it takes a great deal of this sort of courage to say what you know God wants you to say. Do not be afraid to face conflict or stand up against society, yourself, or your universe. This does not mean that you go around picking fights or dragging along your soapbox and turning every meeting place into an arena. It does mean that when you observe a confusion of values or an evidence of wrong directions, you do not fear

to examine the conflict between what you see and what you believe to be right.

Try to peel away the accumulated layers of traditional thought and practice and find what God's Word actually says on an issue. Then, go gently, speak softly, and ask God for the right time and the proper forum for you to share the message you know is vital.

8. *A writer needs a clear assurance of his calling.* Without such assurance when you receive your first rejection slip, you may store your typewriter in the attic. If you are convinced God has called you to write, you will think of yourself as a writer. Such a self-image will make a difference in the way you look at life, the way you plan your schedule, the kinds of things you carry in your purse or pocket. It will enable you to keep your antennae out and your evaluation mechanisms active. Confidence and writer self-image grow with practice. So keep at it.

9. *Finally, if you are to become a producing writer, you will need technical qualifications.* They are:
   a. *A keen imagination.* Regardless of whether you write highly creative poetry or fiction or simple journalistic articles for the neighborhood newspaper, you will need to learn to write in an imaginative way. This involves taking the raw materials of life and arranging and presenting them with sparkle.

   If you do not feel imaginative, try a few exercises to increase creativity. Read creative materials and observe the techniques that make them lively. Ask yourself, "What if?" about a dozen possible situations you could face. Then push your mind in the directions the answers lead you. At first it may take effort. With practice, you can become an expert. One day you may awake to discover in yourself a highly developed imagination.
   b. *An insatiable curiosity.* When you stop asking the question "Why?" you cease to have anything to say. Program yourself to look at everything that happens or everything you see or every idea that suggests itself to you and then

to turn on the question machine: "Where did this come from? What made him do this? How can I be sure this is true? Why?" Develop a voracious appetite for meaning and background information.

We can carry this too far and become nosy. Prying for details, when to share them would not be proper, is rude, even for a writer. Ask God to give you the needed balance to make you godly-wise and compassionate. As you let God sanctify your curiosity, he will use it for constructive good, not for the destruction of persons.

c. *Literary appreciation.* Cultivate a love affair with words and written materials. Many beginning writers long to write profusely, but they have no desire to read. Impossible! Until we expose ourselves to great ideas, great forms, and the wide, rich variety of words and how they are most effectively used, we will be lacking in some of the most important tools available to a writer.

d. *Flexibility and a thick skin.* This is a willingness to experiment and take risks and make changes—even scrap pet projects. It involves learning to separate ourselves from our work and take criticism of the work we have done as simply that, and not as an attack on our persons.

e. *A persistent will to work and a determination never to give up.* Saleable manuscripts do not flow fullblown from an inspired pen. Rather, they are coaxed and cajoled into being, at the cost of emotional blood, agonizing pain, and nagging doubts.

A well-known rule in writing circles is that easy writing makes for difficult reading. The thing you read that moves effortlessly, paints graphic pictures, and stirs a deep emotional response in you was produced by a major struggle in some very human writer. Writing is like childbirth—a long, uncomfortable gestation period with an excruciating birthing, followed by indescribable joy.

f. *Ability to work in solitude.* This means different things to different people. Some can sit at the kitchen table surrounded by childish pandemonium and type away in a cocoon of self-imposed solitude. Others demand total physical isolation in order to get the creative juices flowing. Most of us learn to work in a variety of environmental situations. We all have to learn, however, that writing is a lonely craft. Friends and teachers may give us guidance. A critique group may evaluate what we have written. But we do the actual writing—all alone.

In addition to these qualifications for all writers, each specific type of writing is suited to some people and not to others. Good poetry demands a keenness for color, words, and creativity. Fiction requires a combination of imagination and analytical skills. Journalism calls for people with quick minds, a flair for adventure, and a love for mixing with people.

How will you find where you fit? Take an inventory of yourself, yes. But mostly you will learn by experimentation. Remember that you will never know what you can do well until you try it.

Lesson Three
Part Two
Writing Effective Sentences

Words are the basic building blocks of written expression. In Lesson 2 (Part 2) we learned what words do and how to choose and use them well. If we are to express ourselves meaningfully however, we must also learn to combine them into idea units or sentences.

A *sentence* is a planned cluster of words arranged in such a way that they express a complete thought about some subject. Every sentence must contain two parts—a *subject* (what the sentence is about) and a *predicate* (the actions or state of being of the subject). Neither part standing alone can be called a sentence.
Example:

Subject (not a sentence): The shaggy Airdale dog
Predicate (not a sentence): gobbled down his food
Sentence (subject and predicate): The shaggy Airdale dog gobbled down his food.
This same sentence could be changed to show the state of being, rather than the action of the dog: The shaggy Airdale dog *is a beloved family pet.*

Sentences vary in style, length, content, and construction. No single formula fits all sentences, but all sentences should contain three elements in proper balance:

1. *Clarity,* which makes them understandable. (Sometimes it takes more than one sentence in combination to fully accomplish this.)
2. *Force,* which makes the reader think.
3. *Color,* which makes them interesting.

The writer's imagination and personality combine to give a sentence these three elements.

In this lesson we will discover how to master this combination process. How? By looking at (1) what kinds of sentences confuse readers or put them to sleep, (2) the four basic types of sentences, (3) rules for writing effective sentences, and (4) a special exercise in sentence writing.

SENTENCES WHICH CONFUSE OR BORE READERS

1. *Excessively cluttered sentences.* They lack force and sometimes also clarity and color.
   Example:

   Cluttered: The awesome fact finally dawned upon us all that the abnormal and excessive amounts of snow that poured forth upon us on that unusually chilly afternoon were nothing short of an old-fashioned super-diller of a blizzard.

   Better: As the snowfall intensified, we realized we were in the midst of a blizzard.

   Here are some commonly used, unnecessary qualifying phrases a good writer will avoid:

   I propose to show you that . . .
   It remains to demonstrate that . . .
   It goes without saying that . . .
   There is reason to believe that . . . .

   Also avoid redundant words and phrases such as: sour in taste, reduplication, combine together, hazardous risk, irregardless, interpersonal relationships.

2. *Shoddily constructed sentences.* Lacking clarity, these can be read in more than one way.

Examples:

> Walking down Broadway, the courthouse clock struck twelve.
> "The pedestrian had no idea which way to go, so I ran over him."[2]

3. *Sentences with confused tenses or pronouns.*
   Example (tenses):

   > *Confused:* When she heaved open the heavy door, it creaks and sends shudders down her spine.
   > *Better:* When she heaved open the heavy door, it creaked and sent shudders down her spine.

   Example (pronouns):

   > *Confused:* Opposite us, in our compartment, I felt uncomfortable, as an older woman probed us with her eyes.
   > *Better:* Opposite us in our compartment, an older woman probed us with eyes that made me feel uncomfortable.

4. *Sentences that do not follow each other logically.* Sentences should appear to grow out of one another in a smooth-flowing fashion, so your reader never has to stop and go back to see how they are related to one another.
   Example:

   > Letter from a newspaper boy read: "If you have any problems, just call me. And I will be collecting soon."
   > From a church newsletter: "Congratulations to P. and J. who became Mr. and Mrs. L. this past Saturday evening. There will be an infant dedication on August 10."

5. *Sentences with incorrectly used words.*
   Example:

   > *Incorrect:* He never could *except* her as she was.
   > *Correct:* He never could *accept* her as she was.

Always strive for the precise word that means exactly what you intend to say. If in doubt, look it up in your dictionary or book of usage.

WRITING EFFECTIVE SENTENCES

6. *Dull, ordinary, uninteresting sentences.* Strive to make each sentence sparkle with life and color. Replace generalities with image-evoking specifics. Remember you are painting pictures, not just reporting basic facts.
Example:

> *Dull:* The cat walked down the street.

> (Unanswered questions: What kind of cat? Persian? Tiger? Alley cat? Mother? Black? Kitten? Old tom cat?
> How did he walk? Scamper? Slink? Stalk? Pad?
> What kind of street? Main street? Busy intersection? Dark alley? Residential street? Dirt road? Country lane?
> Where is he going? Stalking a bird? Escaping from an angry dog? Hurrying home?
> What is his mood? Fear? Anticipation of a catch? Confusion in busy traffic?)

Example:

> *Colorful:* Succumbing to an urgent feeling that she was being followed, Melissa turned and gasped to see her grey fluff-ball kitten scampering after her down the noisy city street.

FOUR BASIC TYPES OF SENTENCES

Become familiar with the basic sentence types:

1. *Declarative sentences*—make statements.
Example:

> I tried without success to reach a boy named Jimmy.

2. *Interrogatory sentences*—ask questions.
Example:

> Who dared to suggest such a preposterous idea?

3. *Imperative sentences*—issue commands.
Example:

> Don't fail to call me an hour before dinner.

4. *Exclamatory sentences*—utter exclamations.
Example:

> What a dreadful mess!

Good writers depend mostly on declarative sentences of varying lengths and complexities. But they also learn to handle and insert the other types as well. Proper usage of all four sentence types is essential to create variety, emphasis, color, and clarity.

RULES FOR WRITING EFFECTIVE SENTENCES

1. *Whenever possible, express yourself in simple, direct statements.* Use complex sentences only for variety, color, smoothness, and effect. Never be so complex that you sacrifice clarity.
   Example:

   > *Too complex:* I am dearly endeared to the overwhelmingly superior practice of isolating myself from my busy dizzy world and, shut away in the sweetness of some quiet room shared only with the walls, the furniture, and perhaps an occasional chirping cricket or silent spider, thoroughly enjoying protracted times of treasured, private solitude.
   > *Simple and superior:* I love solitude.

2. *Use the active voice.* Do not meander around the subject before attacking it, when you could better go straight to your point. Let your subject act rather than being acted upon.
   Example:

   > *Passive:* The sweater was knitted by her.
   > *Active:* She knitted the sweater.

   Avoid the use of forms of the verb *to be*, unless to do so makes your sentence either unclear or awkward. Make every *to be* expression defend its existence on the page.
   Example:

68

Poor: The boy watched intently as the dog *was eating* his supper with noisy gulps.

Better: The boy watched intently as the dog *gobbled down* his supper with noisy gulps.

3. *Positive sentences are usually better than negative ones.* Example:

Poor: He almost never came to work on time.

Better: He had a habit of coming late to work.

4. *Vary the length and type of sentences.* Suit the sentence length to the content and pacing of your story. Short sentences give the effect of action and immediacy. Unless they are awkward and cumbersome, longer sentences produce a smoother, more flowing effect.

Use short sentences in a series to produce a fast-paced, efficient, hard-hitting effect.
Example:

"Our grandparents built this hallowed institution. Our parents lived in unquestioning awe of it. But our generation? We form siege lines around it."[3]

A series of short sentences, however, often gives a choppy effect in place of the smooth flow we want.
Example:

The tiger did not answer. He rubbed against his master's leg. He twitched his whiskers. He turned from the man. He lay down beside his mate. She was his true friend.

An artful arrangement of short and long sentences makes for smoother reading. Short sentences properly interspersed with longer ones can heighten emphasis or contrast.
Example:

"But the tiger did not answer. He only rubbed against his master once more, twitched his whiskers, and lay down beside his mate on the lush grass."[4]

5. *Use concrete statements in place of abstract ones.* Show a concept in action; do not give it a name tag.

Example:

> *Abstract:* Dick was in a big hurry to get to church.
>
> *Concrete:* "Dick gulped down the last of his coffee, grabbed his Bible and headed for the door, shouting, 'Come on kids! Time to run.'"[5]

6. *Make your sentences clear and logical.* Never force your reader to reread a sentence in order to be certain of its meaning.
Example:

> *Confusing:* To write a good article, many adult education courses are available.
>
> *Clear:* Many adult education courses are available to help the beginner learn to write a good article.

7. *Remember that the most important words of your sentence belong at the beginning and the end.* Save relatively non-essential words for the middle of your sentences.

When you want to arrest attention, place your most important words at the beginning of the sentence.
Example:

> *"The dream soon turned into a nightmare,* though, as Wally's regular work duties increased, and the load fell more and more on me."[6]

When you want to build up to a point and present it as the climax of a thought, use the most important words at the end of the sentence.
Example:

> While business was not my first love, *I determined to make a success of it.*[7]

8. *Arrange your sentences in such a way that they say precisely what you intend them to say.* Put the emphasis where it belongs, in order to make your point.
Example:

> *Wrong:* Esther noticed how, one by one, their animated conversations stopped all around her *with growing uneasiness.*

Right: "With growing uneasiness, Esther noticed how, one by one, their animated conversations stopped all around her."[8]

A SPECIAL EXERCISE IN SENTENCE WRITING: THE CRAPSEY CINQUAIN

One of the best ways I have found to practice writing sentences that fulfill all the requirements we have talked about is to learn to write the Crapsey Cinquain. It is a five-line poem invented by Adelaide Crapsey. Each line consists of a given number of syllables. Here is a sample:

Give me
a tender eye—
sensitive to sin-smog
with quivery lids, unashamed
to weep.[9]

Rules for writing a Crapsey Cinquain:
1. Syllable count is as follows:
   Line 1—two
   Line 2—four
   Line 3—six
   Line 4—eight
   Line 5—two
2. It contains one simple thought expressed in a more or less complete sentence.
3. It eliminates all unnecessary words (*and, but, the,* and other connectives). Use such words only if needed for clarity, rhythm, or special effect. Never use them to increase syllable count.
4. Its statement flows cohesively from one line to the next.
5. It is based on the use of image-evoking, emotion-producing words and phrases.
6. Avoid the use of rhyme, if possible, unless it would enhance the effect you want to create.

Procedure for writing a Crapsey Cinquain (with example)
1. Write a simple sentence, expressing the one thing you want to say.

Example:

> The late summer storm shatters the dark sky with a streak of lightning and a clap of deafening thunder.

2. Search for a two-syllable first line.
Example:

> Silver or Lightning

3. Experiment and write specifically, picturesquely.
Example: (Rough draft)

> *Lightning*
> *slices leaden*
> *snow-pregnant cloud mantle*
> *then shakes expectant stillness with*
> *thunder.*

4. Check it for:
   a. *Smoothness:* Does it flow easily from line to line?
   b. *Tense agreement:* Have you mixed past with present?
   c. *Syllable count:* Is this accurate?
   d. *Unnecessary words:* Have you inserted useless connectives that weaken the impact of your poem?
   e. *Repetition:* Have you repeated words throughout? This poem is too small to allow for repetition, unless needed for special effect or unless to use a synonym would make the sound or sense awkward.
   f. *Unity:* Do you have one idea only? If you have attempted to put too many ideas into one cinquain, maybe you can do a series of cinquains as stanzas in a longer poem.
5. Include a title only if needed. Titles are considered to be an integral part of poems, though they are not to be included in the line syllable count. Keep them short and tie them to the interpretation of your poems.
Example: (for rough draft example above)

> *SUMMER CAESAREAN*

6. Polish and rearrange words to make this represent your best effort.
Example:

SUMMER CAESAREAN

Silver
lightning slices
leaden snow-pregnant cloud
then shakes expectant stillness with
thunder.

ASSIGNMENT

1. Rewrite the following sentences so they are not dull and general, but lively, colorful, and specific.
   a. The girl chose a dress.
   b. The wind blew the sign.
   c. The man ate his dinner.
   d. The boy fell from the tree.
2. Write a Crapsey Cinquain, following the above rules and procedures.

[1] Reuel Howe, *Creative Years* (New York: Seabury Press, Inc., 1959), p. 60.

[2] *Have a Good Day,* July 1979, p. 1.

[3] Ethel Herr, *Schools: How Parents Can Make a Difference* (Chicago: Moody Press, 1981), p. 15.

[4] Ethel Herr, *Chosen Families of the Bible* (Chicago: Moody Press, 1981), p. 13.

[5] Ethel Herr, "Is There a Camel in Your Tent?" *Eternity,* January 1977, p. 40.

[6] Ethel Herr, "Slow Down and Live," *Scope,* March 1974, p. 18.

[7] Ibid.

[8] Ethel Herr, *Chosen Families,* p. 99.

[9] Ethel Herr, Untitled, *Decision,* October 1980, p. 15.

Lesson Four
Part One
How Do I Get Ready to Write?

To become a writer means serving a long apprenticeship. One simply does not awaken one morning with the inspiration to become a writer who picks up a golden pen and starts a career that blossoms overnight. Rather, he expends an incredible amount of energy, encounters frustrations and discouragements. In spite of the bright and glowing moments and indescribable satisfactions along the way, he soon learns that becoming a writer demands a "til-death-do-us-part" level of commitment.

How do we prepare to have something to say and also develop an inner feel for, and understanding of, the literary process, thereby enabling us to say it well?

First, we must all struggle to grow consistently in our relationship with the Lord. A neglected spiritual life will kill our writing ministry because it always leads to an empty heart and surface conclusions about the challenges of life. Further, it makes the writer vulnerable to writing for the wrong reasons, leading him to adopt erroneous viewpoints.

Second, we need to develop right attitudes. This means worshiping God through our lives and ministries via the printed page. We must remember that we are servants in search of a place to minister rather than performers courting a reputation or men's applause. It is crucial that we remain positive, rejecting the idea of any possibility of ultimate failure in our work. That means we must guard against fatalistic and pessimistic attitudes and expectations in life. We are ministers of hope, not prophets of gloom. Developing a right attitude also means being willing to experiment and take risks. As long as we continue to grow in the Lord, risks and experiments will not threaten us. Rather they will entice us as they provide opportunities to sink the roots of our confidence deeper into the God whom we serve.

Third, we need to gain a practical working knowledge of English grammar. Because this is a complete subject in itself and because many excellent books are available to help you brush up on your grammar, I am not attempting to cover it in this book. If you have not looked at grammar in a long time or if you know it to be one of your weak areas, make the time to take a college or an adult education course to help bring you up to performance level. Otherwise you could purchase and study one of the inexpensive books in the book list at the end of this lesson.

Fourth, we need to develop good reading habits. The primary area we will be considering in this lesson is that of *reading*. When I work with high school writing students, I am always amazed at their illogical expectations. They want to write great manuscripts, but they do not want to spend any time reading great works. This attitude betrays an immaturity that will slow down the learning process. If we are unwilling to read, we will be unable to write well.

WHAT READING ACCOMPLISHES

Reading does several things for a writer.

First, it causes him to grow as a person and to expand his own personal outlook on life. Lillian Smith has said that "growth comes only through contact with what is larger and greater than oneself—something to 'stretch' the mind and give direction to the imagination. . . ."[1] Reading does for the mind what exercise does for the body. It keeps us from becoming flabby, stiff, obese, and dull.

Horace Mann once said, "A house without books is like a room without windows."[2] If we are to grow, we need literary windows to expose us to the vast world of knowledge and ideas. We need our points of view challenged, expanded, sometimes even altered. Reading is one of the best ways to do this.

Second, reading helps the writer to discover the needs of potential readers. Editors make a scientific study of readers' needs and plan their magazines, newspapers, and book lists accordingly. You will learn to understand the people you hope to reach by reading the articles, books, stories, and poems that they read. Notice also the titles (carefully crafted to arrest their attention) and letters they write to editors.

Third, reading enables the writer to become familiar with editorial needs. I have been told that as many as 50 percent of unsolicited manuscripts received by the average magazine can be rejected simply because they are the wrong subject for that magazine. Studying the magazines will give you an educated feel for the kinds of writing each one buys. It will also help you isolate the topics they have already covered so well that they no longer need to buy any more material on those topics. It takes hardly any more time and money to read your target magazines than to write unpublishable manuscripts and submit them.

Fourth, reading serves as a means of research for writing. It is a rare piece of writing you will do which will not require you to do some book and/or magazine research, even if it means only verifying a fact or looking up a word.

Fifth, reading often gives the writer new ideas for future projects. If you read an article in the newspaper about a new archeological discovery in one of the Bible lands, it may arouse your curiosity so that you start studying the subject to learn more for yourself and maybe share your findings in an article. Perhaps an article in the newspaper took an antibiblical stand; you will examine the evidence carefully and give the world a biblical position. Something else you read may remind you of an experience worth sharing. Other items make you aware that certain relationship problems you have solved are more common than you suspected. So you decide to share your experience and helpful insights.

Sixth, reading gives the writer a good understanding of the many sides of an issue. When you read a strong article which presents a controversial topic reflecting your point of view assign yourself the task of finding articles that take opposing positions as well.

Purposely challenging your thinking will do one of several things. It may reaffirm and help you to verbalize the position from which you started. It may help you to see that your position was erroneous and needs some changing. Or it may convince you that the issue is not as simple as you had once thought and deserves a great deal more research before you state your feelings dogmatically. Every writer needs these kinds of mind-stretching exercises to keep him flexible, alert, and believable.

Seventh, reading provides an excellent source of material. With it, the writer can observe and begin to absorb writing techniques and style. Every writer needs some reference books—dictionaries, quotation books, and the like (more about these in Lesson 6). However, there is nothing like a written model to teach us about technique and style. Someone has said that "every book is a silent lesson from one writer to another."[3] Writing is an ancient craft that has developed gradually over the years. Writers learn from each other, both what should be done and what should be avoided. The richer our background of literary knowledge, the richer our store from which to draw when we are developing our expertise as writers.

Finally, reading encourages and inspires writers to write. Often when I begin to read truly great writing, my initial reaction is,

"Oh, no, I can never reach that standard of excellence, so what makes me think I ought to try?" Invariably, by the time I have finished the book or poem, something inside me is itching to get at my typewriter. I feel that I have walked with a giant and heard his words of inspiration urging me on to follow in his steps.

Having considered what reading does for us, we need to be aware of three dangers and how to avoid them:

1. that we spend all our time reading and never make time to write.
2. that we not read in the correct way to learn what we need to learn.
3. that we fail to make wise reading choices.

How much time should a writer spend reading? When I was about to make the transition from a hobby writer to a part-time professional free-lancer, I went through a near-nervous breakdown caused by overcommitment. Since the doctor pre-scribed large doses of rest, I began reading everything I could lay my hands on, while I rested. Such fun! Then, one day I awoke to realize that if I was ever going to make that important transition as a writer, I had to start limiting my reading and do the disciplined thing—take time to write.

A good rule to follow is to read as much as you can and still make time to write and experience life. This means different things to different people. One man sets a schedule for him-self—reading a minimum of 100 pages of fiction per day and examining 30 magazines and newspapers a week for trends and ideas. A poetry teacher once told us to read at least 100 poems for every one we tried to write. These are mechanical formulae, and they don't work for all of us in the same way. Set your goals; then experiment to find what best meets your needs, temperament, and family schedule.

Two important things will help you to design your reading plan:

1. Develop a reading-environment mentality. As Catherine Drinker Bowen says of a biographer, "Print is his habitat, he swims in it like a fish in a river."[4] Position books and maga-zines that you want to read in many places throughout your

house. Make reading material always readily available so you can fill many of your tiny chinks of unstructured time with profitable reading.

2. Be careful not to let reading take the place of thinking. Also schedule some time to be quiet and reflect, to write in your journal, to absorb what you read.

What is the right way to read in order to maximize the benefits? Let me suggest the following four steps:

1. Read a piece through for the overall idea. When you finish, it may be helpful to write a *synopsis* —a summary of the idea structure of the piece in capsule form.

2. Reread the piece with a pencil in hand. If the book or magazine is your own, mark it. Underline, circle words, draw arrows and lines. In the margins, write topics, outlines, and reactions. Otherwise, use a notebook to record ideas, words, style notations, situations, ways to improve your own work, sentence and paragraph treatments, new word meanings, errors you want to avoid. Take special note of effective and weak beginnings, endings, transitions, word usage, and characterizations.

3. You may reread one more time and analyze it in depth. Look for the deep meaning, the world view. As James Sire suggests in his book *How To Read Slowly,* look for:
   a. An idea of God or ultimate reality.
   b. An idea of essential nature of the external world. Is it ordered or chaotic? Material or spiritual?
   c. An idea of who man is. What is human nature?
   d. An understanding of ethics.
   e. An idea of the meaning of history.[5]
   Study how the writer has communicated these points of view of the world. Notice how he states his concepts, how he uses details to support them, and how he appeals to the reader to act in accordance with his thesis.

4. Write an evaluation of what you have read. Record how you felt about it. Was it well-written? Significant? Positive? Helpful? Thought-provoking? Did the author fulfill any expectations he gave you? Was his authority good? Was he accurate? Careful? Would you recommend the book or article to others?

Finally, how can the Christian writer make wise reading choices? At the end of this section is a detailed list of books I feel every writer should read and some other lists from which you should choose, depending on the type of writing you plan to do. However, you will need some guidelines for choosing reading materials not directly related to your writing.

1. Read widely. Vary the kinds of materials, subjects, and points of view you read. Do not limit yourself to your denominational magazine or read only fiction or poetry or biographies. Make a reading plan that encompasses both Christian and non-Christian points of view, in many literary forms.

2. Include the classics on your list. Books that have endured for many years have a quality that makes them worthy of our careful attention. However, their style may be terribly out of date. Do not read Dickens and Harriet Beecher Stowe with the intention of copying their style. Reading these works does expose us to depths of characterization, technique, and idea content that will help us to do a better job in modern style.

3. Read daily newspapers and weekly news magazines. Keep up with current events. As you are reading, notice the commercials. How do businesses sell themselves to the public? These things provide a helpful index to the needs and characters of readers that open them up to new ideas, such as yours. Read sketches about people facing problems and interacting with one another. This is a rich source of education in human nature and a gold mine of idea starters. Observe the trends in thinking and public awareness. Know the world you are living in and attempting to communicate with.

4. Read authors who write as you would like to write. Avoid those who write poorly. Build an admiration file of works and authors you enjoy and who write well. We have all been told that we become what we eat. Similarly, we tend to write in a manner or on a level of expertise comparable to that of the things we read.

5. Read biographies of other writers. Read stories of how writers came to write their books. Read interviews with writers. If you are like me, you are insatiably curious about what makes other writers tick and motivates them to write the things they do. If I never read another thing in a book, I always

read the introduction or preface and jacket cover. I want to know where it came from and how the author felt or looked at life.

6. Read and study the Bible. Of all the suggestions I have given you, none surpasses this one in importance. Master it. You must become a Bible expert. It will take you a lifetime. No matter how many changes you make in your reading plans, plug your Bible in as the perpetual top priority study for the rest of your life. Nothing will prepare you better than this.

Lesson Four
Part Two
Writing Strong
Paragraphs

Effective writing begins with observations and ideas expressed in the symbols we call *words*. These words transfer meaning as they are placed in sequence as sentences. Sentences, in turn, must also be grouped together to form paragraphs which become the basic structural units of unified written thought.

Because the paragraph is the simplest component of writing that must embody all the characteristics of well-developed, properly ordered, cohesive, and colorful expression, every good writer needs to take time to master its composition. In the words of prominent historiographer Louis Gottschalk, "If once one learns to quarry a humble block of stone, one can hope someday to build a great cathedral."[6] Since we are preparing to erect magnificent cathedrals to serve as meeting places between God and man, we need to learn to quarry some humble blocks of written stone—paragraphs.

THE PARAGRAPH

It is a cohesive group of sentences which develops a single idea and supports that idea with details.

THE FUNCTIONS OF THE PARAGRAPH

1. The paragraph breaks up the visual appearance of the printed page and increases legibility.
2. The paragraph helps the reader to organize ideas and their relationship to one another in clear, logical ways.
3. The paragraph sometimes stands alone as a complete message (filler material).
   Example:

   "Think of it! If light were never fractured, there would be no rainbows. And, by the same measure, if our lives were never broken, we would never see the splendour of one another's humanity. It's that simple. Thank God for the times that try our souls."[7]

4. For the writer, paragraphs are manageable blocks of stone that provide valuable exercise to help develop your cathedral-building skills.

THE DIFFERENT KINDS OF PARAGRAPHS

Paragraphs are divided according to their specific functions in a story or article. (Note: Unless otherwise noted, the remainder of the examples in this lesson are taken from the article "Is There a Camel in Your Tent?" on pages 239 – 244.)

1. *Narrative Paragraphs.* These tell a story in sequence.
   Example:

   "Dick and Marcia never intended to overcommit themselves. But they loved the Lord, wanted to serve Him, and had listened to a lot of sermons on the parable of the talents. Once they identified the problem, they did some hard figuring and praying about priorities. Then they marched off to the powers that sat in the church office and handed in a few long-overdue resignations."

2. *Logical Sequence Paragraphs.* These develop an idea logically.
   Example:

   "First is the myth that church activity is always service. If we are active in church work, we are 'obviously' serving the Lord. And if we want to serve the Lord, we must 'obviously' get ourselves involved up to the eyeballs in church work."

3. *Explanatory Paragraphs.* State a thesis. Then explain it by logic or support it with quotes, facts, illustrations.
Example:

Explain by logic: "God's will is not always externally obvious. But it is discernible. Many things figure into God's plan for us. Things like our own personal growth, the community where we live, current social trends and many more. As we learn to focus on God intimately, we can discover which talents he's scheduled for development today."

Example:

Support with a quote: "A fourth myth hits us all at a vulnerable point. It is the God-will-give-you-strength-to-do-anything argument. One pastor put it this way: 'I get the feeling that our evangelical culture has conditioned us quite well to conclude that "God who is our refuge and strength" will provide the strength to run ourselves to a frazzle.'"

4. *Descriptive Paragraphs.* These describe a setting (place, mood or situation, often with something happening).
Example:

"At 4:30 on a grayish Sunday afternoon, Dick and Marcia sat down to a cup of strong coffee. Dick yawned. Marcia stared into her steaming handcrafted mug."

5. *Comparison and/or Contrast Paragraphs.* These use comparison and/or contrast to support a thesis.
Example:

"While activity is not always wrong, it is not necessarily service to God. Obedience to individual guidance, on the other hand, will always be a service to Jesus Christ. This may take the form of ringing doorbells for the Heart Fund or local school bond issue. It may mean sitting very still to worship or simply enjoying a bicycle ride, a sunset or a jig-saw puzzle. Our first service to God is to become all he wants us to become, letting him form in us his own image, for the *world* (not just our church co-workers) to see."

EFFECTIVE PARAGRAPHS

Good paragraphs will invariably possess the following qualities:

1. *Clarity.* Does the paragraph make sense? Is your intention absolutely clear to your reader? Clarity is attained by the use of clear, accurate words arranged in proper sequence into sentences which have been combined in just the right order.

2. *Force.* Does the paragraph make any difference? Does it offer some significant thought to your reader? Or does it leave the reader asking, "So what?" Force is accomplished by the use of precise, active, colorful words and sentences arranged in such a way that the reader is carried along irresistibly. End your paragraph with a punch. Never let a paragraph die out gradually, unless for some special effect.

   Max Gunther says of good paragraphs: "The reader has been pulled into one end of the paragraph and pushed out the other."[8]

3. *Unity.* Does the paragraph have one thought only? Does every sentence in the paragraph contribute to that thought either as a statement, support, or setting? Most paragraphs contain a topic sentence which summarizes the thesis. This is not always necessary, however. Unity is attained by eliminating extraneous materials and arranging thoughts in a logical way so that they seem to flow and the reader never has to stop and reread a paragraph to see where you the writer are leading him.
   Example:

   Poor and disconnected: I've had many painful experiences with overcommitment. Not all jobs people think are important in the Church are God's idea. Having many talents is as problematic to deal with as having no easily recognized ones. Just because there is no one to do the job doesn't mean I have to do it.

Better:

Pared and restructured: "After many painful experiences with overcommitment, I've concluded that if in reality there is no one to do a job, maybe it doesn't need to be done. At any rate, I'm not responsible to do the whole work of the Body of Christ, not even in my local church."

PARAGRAPH LENGTH

Paragraph lengths vary. This lends variety and helps to keep the reader's attention. A paragraph may be as short as a single word, particularly in dialogue passages. Many paragraphs are single sentences which serve as transitions between other paragraphs and ideas. Others may run up to 500 words or more.

Lengths vary with:

1. Type of material. For example, textbooks may use long complex paragraphs. Dialogue employs short paragraphs. Narration varies lengths.
2. Effect the writer wishes to create. For example, quick action is presented in short choppy sentences and paragraphs. Smooth-flowing narrative depends on longer paragraphs. Scholarly material may go into very long paragraphs.
3. Intellectual level of your target audience.

General rule for paragraph length: Aim for the average reader and use mostly short paragraphs of 125 words or less.

GUIDELINES FOR COMPOSING
EFFECTIVE PARAGRAPHS

1. Vary length and type of sentences within your paragraph. Using all short declarative sentences makes a dull paragraph. Using all simple sentences makes for choppy reading. Using all complex sentences discourages the reader. When it comes to sentence length, it is more than a worn cliché to say that variety is the spice of life.

2. *Put emphasis in the right place for effect and clarity.* A strong statement at the beginning reaches out and grabs the reader and draws him in immediately. A strong statement sometimes fits better at the conclusion, particularly when you need to prepare the reader to accept what you have to say.

3. *Most paragraphs contain a topic sentence,* which expresses a central thought and is supported by other sentences. (Note: Sentences below in italics are *topic* sentences.)
   a. Usually the topic sentence comes at or near the beginning.
      Example:

      "The result is that many Christians resemble a child on a coin-operated horse at the supermarket. As long as the coin holds out, they go like crazy, generating tremendous activity. But they don't get anywhere. When the coins run out, they're still sitting where they started."

   b. Sometimes the topic sentence comes in the middle.
      Example:

      "God gives us strength for those things he designs for us to do. *If we are running out of energy, we need to evaluate ourselves, our dreams and our schedules.* Let's weed out the God-wants-me-to's from the I'd-surely-love-to's."

   c. Often the topic sentence comes at the end.
      Example:

      "Have you ever experienced the pains of spreading yourself too thin, while using every talent? Have you known the frustration of trying to pick and choose between a dozen delightful talent options, all of which match your qualifications and interests precisely? Then you know that this myth just isn't so! *Having too many talents can pose just as many problems as having no talents—sometimes even more."*

General rule for proper placement of the topic sentence: Place the topic sentence where it will have the most impact on the reader and make itself most memorable.

ASSIGNMENT:

1. Outline a reading plan for the next month. Include daily readings, Bible study, and longer projects.
2. Examine the Paragraph Study Sheet containing sentences turned into paragraphs. Count the number of words per paragraph. Count the number of words per sentence in each paragraph. Underline the topic sentence and note where it is located in the paragraph.
3. Using your own rewritten sentences from Lesson 3 (Part 2), expand each one into a paragraph of not more than 125 words. Remember that each single paragraph need not tell a whole story, but will comprise a complete unit of thought for some larger story.

[1] Lillian Smith, *The Unreluctant Years* (Chicago: American Library Association, 1953), p. 38.

[2] Kaehele, *Sealed Orders*, p. 24.

[3] *Famous Writers Course*, Famous Writers School, 1969 Vol. 2, p. 525.

[4] Catherine Drinker Bowen, *Biography: The Craft and the Calling* (Westport CT: Greenwood Press, 1978), p. 157.

[5] James Sire, *How To Read Slowly* (Downers Grove IL: InterVarsity Press, 1978), p. 14.

[6] Louis Gottschalk, *Understanding History* (New York: Alfred A. Knopf, 1961), p. 66.

[7] John Killinger, Untitled, *Alive Now,* Nov/Dec 1975, p. 11.

[8] Max Gunther, *Writing and Selling a Non-Fiction Book* (Cincinnati: The Writer,* 1973), p. 76.

PARAGRAPH STUDY SHEET_____

Examples of sentences turned into paragraphs:

1. *Simple sentence:* The boy went into the house.
   Expanded sentence: "Silently the small boy slipped inside one of the side doors to the great house."
   Paragraph: "Silently the small boy slipped inside one of the side doors to the great house. He listened. No sound. Glancing down at his strawberry-stained hands and arms, he rubbed them on his light blue jacket."[9]

2. *Simple sentence:* The girl gave the woman a slip of paper.
   Expanded sentence: "My seven-year-old handed me her much pondered list, which was erased, scratched out, and scrawled in half print/half cursive."
   Paragraph: "My seven-year-old handed me her much pondered list, which was erased, scratched out, and scrawled in half print/half cursive. But my smiles soon turned to tears as I read a most surprising request—for a grandmother—and the wavy slanting line that followed, 'I get to chooz her out miself.'"[10]

3. *Simple sentence:* We planted a tree.
   Expanded sentence: "Tenderly we lifted it from its native ridge and bore it down beside the lake."
   Paragraph: "The last tree planted during our first season was a golden-needled larch from the high hills. Cheri and I made a special trip to the high country, just to pick one out. Tenderly we lifted it from its high ridge and bore it down beside the lake. It stands erect at the water's edge. If all goes well, its feathery form and golden needles will enhance 'Still Waters' for a hundred years to come."[11]

[9] Dave Collins, "White-House Wild-Cat," *Climb*, Feb. 6, 1972, p. 5.

[10] Betty Biesterveld, "The Wish List," *Sunday Digest*, June 10, 1973, p. 8.

[11] Phillip Keller, *Still Waters* (Old Tappan NJ: Fleming H. Revell Co., 1980), p. 45.

Lesson Five
Part One
Can I Stick with It?

Many people dream of *being* writers. Relatively few ever invest the necessary time and energy to *become* writers. As you no doubt have already discovered, becoming a writer involves a lot of writing. As with any other kind of art, mastering the literary art takes work. It demands a relentless dedication to consistent exercise of the craft that combines ideas with words and wrestles clear, pleasant communication onto the blank page.

For all who want to become writers, here is a set of time-tested essentials—what I call my Writer's Daily Dozen Disciplines.

1. *Understand the creative cycle.* Creativity is a tricky thing. Because at times it seems to come more easily than at others, we tend to feel that we can write well only when the "Spirit moves" us. Not so. Creativity runs in cycles. When we understand these cycles, we can learn to cooperate with them and work in different ways at different points in the cycle, and even short-circuit a couple of unproductive spots in the normal cycle. Briefly, the cycle goes something like this:

a. *A restless urge to write* something, anything, usually nothing in particular. This is the "I-feel-I-must-become-a-writer" stage.

b. *Specific inspiration.* An idea strikes you and you now know what you want to write about. The disciplined writer takes notes fast and furiously at this point. But unless he is doing something such as an intensely personal piece of poetry, he resists the temptation to write his article or story yet.

c. *Research.* This is an essential stage, as we will discuss in Lesson 7 (Part 2). Without it, your writing will lack the substance and/or authenticity to make it significant enough to share.

d. *Organization.* Once you have collected all your materials, organize them into a logical form (See Lesson 8, Part 2).

e. *Rough Draft.* Remember that what you first write from your outline is rough and will need polishing (See Lessons 9 and 10, Part 2).

f. *Cooling-Off: Phase 1.* Set aside your freshly composed rough draft and refuse to look at it for a week. All manuscripts need this incubation period if we are to look at them objectively (See Lesson 11).

g. *Revision.* Now take it out, reread it, and begin to make changes (See Lesson 11, Part 2).

h. *Critique.* When you have done all you know to do, take your manuscript to your critique group and get their suggestions (See Appendix 8).

i. *Evaluation and further revision.* Evaluate all the reactions of your critique group, and make changes accordingly.

j. *Cooling-Off: Phase 2.* Let it cool for a week once more.

k. *Final revision, typing, and submission* (See Lesson 11, Part 2).

l. *Reflection.* Once you have slid the large manila envelope into the mailbox, one of two things will happen. Either your emotions will experience a tremendous infatuation with your brainchild and fill you with visions of its virtues and coming publication, or your mind will retrieve it and begin to pick it apart once more. Do not allow yourself to spend any time with this stage. Short-circuit these problems by moving immediately to another project (See Lesson 11, Part 1).

m. *Dormancy.* Unchecked reflection and/or failure to get involved in another project can be deadly and lead to that stage all writers dread—*writer's block.* At times, such spells are inevitable. If they happen, learn to make creative use of them by pushing your mind and heart into deeper and deeper areas of idea-pursuing and attitude-formation.

2. *Bury all excuses.*
   Examples:

> "I'm too old" or "I'm too young."
> "I don't feel inspired."
> "My family demands all my time and attention."
> "I can't find any solitude."
> "I'm not very original."
> "I'm too busy."

Dreamers make excuses for not *being* writers. People who become writers have to defy the handy alibis available in every person's life. If you are a writer and this is God's time for you to produce, there is no such thing as an excuse that will keep you from your typewriter. Only you and/or God can shoulder the responsibility for your failure to write.

3. *Do not be in a rush to get published.* Remember these two principles:

   (1) Writers must expect to serve a long apprenticeship. Bernard DeSoto once said, "It takes ten years of terrible discipline at the desk for a writer to learn to say things clearly." You may not take that long to be published, but without a great deal of practice, you will never polish your skill.

   (2) Most beginning writers start writing too soon. There is an old familiar saying that a good idea must simmer in its own juices for weeks and months, sometimes even years, before it is ready to be served on paper. Even though the

subject you are writing about may require years of research, thought, and prayer; give it as many years as it demands. Never sacrifice substance for immediacy.

4. *Give your writing a top priority.* One of the shortest words in the English language is one we learn earliest as children and abandon most quickly as adults. It is the simple word *no.* Learn to use it. When you start applying it to the myriad of requests to do things that would keep you from your desk, you may be amazed to find that the world does not collapse for lack of your pillar-holding.

Paul Tournier reminds us so aptly:

> To live is to choose. Those who through a childish notion of what fullness implies want to lose none of their human inheritance, sacrifice nothing, give up nothing, lose out in spreading themselves too thin. They never attain true fullness.[1]

Set aside a specific time and place to write, and keep your commitment. The important thing is not how long you work each day, but how consistently you work. Most books and articles are written on less than three hours a day; many on an hour a day or less. Pick the time that is best for you and your family; then stick to it.

5. *Become a habitual writer.* Reach the point where your mind is always involved in some way, in your writing. Madeleine L'Engle speaks of this discipline as her "writing mind, which is always at work, no matter what is happening on the surface level."[2] When you are physically doing what my sister-in-law calls dumb work (ironing, vacuuming, standing in line), turn your mind to plan, think, research, organize facts, dream, and imagine. Habitual writers write something every day—a letter, a journal entry, research, idea notes, or manuscript drafts. Even if you are not doing a rough draft or revising a manuscript, discipline yourself to put some words on paper every day that you are alive.

6. *Rough-draft profusely.* Master your fear of the blank sheet of paper by writing on it. Do not worry about word limits or

cutting ideas as you rough-draft. Put all your thoughts down. It is much easier to go through later and cut out superfluous materials than to have to insert explanations which, as you wrote the rough draft, you assumed your reader understood. When ideas are flowing easily from your mind and through your fingers, do not stop that magic. Keep at it. On days when the flow is less full, prod it. Entice inspiration into existence. Again, keep at it.

7. *Rewrite ruthlessly.* Good literature is never written. It is re-re-written. Those things that oozed so effortlessly from your inspired pen will usually either lull your reader to sleep or confuse him. Remind yourself that your typewriter does not chisel words into immortal stone. No matter how choice they seem at the wonder-moment of conception, they are almost certain to need polishing, cutting, rewriting.

8. *Learn to concentrate.* Some people naturally need more solitude for creative production than others. Usually you can arrange your writing schedule to coincide with the quiet spots in your life. Manage as many factors of your environment as possible in order to increase your efficiency. If you are like me, you will find that the rhythm of music interferes with the rhythm of what you write, and you will plan to write without music playing. On the other hand, you may find music increases your creative potential. If so, use it.

    At times, all of us lose the ability to control our environment. However, when this happens, it will take more than that to stop you—if you are determined to write. We can all train our determined minds to greater powers of concentration.

9. *Discover the tricks that help you the most.* As you work, you will develop your own set of these. To begin with, here are a few that help many writers:
   a. Act like a professional. Do not apologize for your work, but treat it as a truly important ministry for the King.
   b. Keep pencil and paper by your bedside. Scientific research has proven that many of our best creative inspira-

tions come to us just as we are dozing off to sleep. Never trust your memory to return those gems to you in the morning. Rouse yourself when the idea hits, and get it down THEN.

c. Dress comfortably and neatly when you write. This is part of maintaining a professional attitude and self-image, and will affect your ability to work well.

d. Keep needed books and supplies handy, so you do not waste time hunting for them.

e. Learn to use self-starting methods. If a blank page paralyzes your mind at the beginning of a writing session, start filling it with a description of the scene outside your window, a letter to a friend, a copy of the contents of a book or article. I often begin by typing up a previously composed letter or manuscript. The act of typing soon clears my brain and starts the momentum I am looking for.

f. Set deadlines for yourself. Discover what kind of deadlines work best for you. Some writers insist on writing for so many hours a day. Others will not quit until they have completed a given number of manuscript pages. If you work best under pressure, be merciless with yourself. If pressure destroys your creativity, then find what does prod you to produce.

g. Avoid superstitious practices. I have heard of writers who would not write without a certain pair of slacks or a specific pencil or until the house was spotless. Such things destroy productivity. What happens if the pants fall apart, the dog chews up your pencil, or the house never gets clean enough to suit you? Learn to take full responsibility for your writing performance rather than keeping handy scapegoats for your nonperformance.

h. Take coffee and exercise breaks. The value of those is well acknowledged in every other area of society. They are particularly essential to those of us with sedentary occupations. Learn the frequency and kind of breaks you need. Then set yourself a schedule and live by it.

10. *Pray over all your projects.* Pray at every stage of the creative cycle—before the idea, during the writing, after it is in

the mailbox. Treat it as the God-directed ministry you know it to be. Apply to your writing this advice I heard years ago: Never attempt anything for God that you do not saturate with prayer.

11. *Do not let either the praise or the criticism of unknowledgeable critics influence you.* Perhaps all your aunts, uncles, cousins, children, best friends, and fellow church members love your poetry and are convinced it should be published. Hold on. Remember that does not mean it has sufficient substance, uniqueness, or literary merit to make it publishable. By the same token, neither should you give up just because your spouse does not get excited about your latest brainchild. Be cautious where you go for criticism and praise. Learn to listen to all that your unauthorized critics offer, but consider the sources and never take them as final authorities.

12. *Remind yourself daily of your writing gift.* Be a disciple—a learner under discipline. An excellent verse to memorize and/or hang over your desk is Isaiah 50:4:

> The Lord has given Me the tongue of disciples That I may know how to sustain the weary one with a word. He awakens Me morning by morning, He awakens My ear to listen as a disciple. (NASB)

> *Are you in earnest?*
> *Seize this very minute!*
> *What you can do, or dream you can, begin it!*
> *Boldness has genius, power and magic in it.*
> *Only engage, and then the mind grows heated.*
> *BEGIN, and then the work will be completed.*
> —Goethe[3]

Lesson Five
Part Two
Finding and
Using Ideas

We have noted that good writing begins with clear thinking, which in turn begins with alert observing. But as we observe our world, not all the impressions we collect are worth writing about. What is the difference between an observation and a usable idea? Where can we go to find ideas? How can we evaluate those ideas and focus them to catch the reader's attention and minister to his hurts and longings?

An observation becomes an idea when it can be stated in a significant theme. I observe a colorful wildflower in the field. I ponder it in wonder over its magnificent beauty and exquisite fragility. I think about the incredible way that the God of the universe has invested so much of his creative energy in that small, short-lived fragrant blossom. *An idea emerges:* If God cares enough for that tiny, obscure flower—that is here today and gone tomorrow—to put a bit of himself in it, how much more does he long to fill my eternal life with himself for the whole world to see and enjoy? With such a theme, I am ready to write my poem.

CREATOR'S DELIGHT

I made you   lovely one
delicate
wind-kissed blossom.
Let me waft My fragrance
through your tissue petals
over shimmering fields
of grass. . . .[4]

Not everything a Christian writer writes needs to be Christian in subject matter. We are not called to write simply as spreaders of propaganda, but as artistic ministers. When I write a poetic response to a picture of a mother and child embracing under a wide gold umbrella in a spring rain shower, I need not mention God in order for the poem to be Christian. I must, however, portray the scene with an attitude and point of view that are consistent with God's attitude and point of view. I use it as a means to comment on how God sees his world and the relationships of his human creatures—an exquisite reflection of the Father-Son relationship within the Trinity. The two poems below are equally Christian, even though the first does not mention God:

MOTHER —DAUGHTER AFFAIR

Rubbing
dampish noses
under gold umbrella,
we share treasured moment of Spring
wonder.

BALANCE

Thank God
for
endless creativity
and
man's reflecting image—
receptivity!

Note: For an excellent treatment of this subject, I urge you to read Leland Ryken's *Triumphs of the Imagination* (See booklist on page 235).

FINDING IDEAS ABOUT WHICH TO WRITE

Ideas are everywhere—in all we see, hear, read, touch, experience, do, feel, and learn about. The secret, as with observation, is to keep your antennae tuned in to all of life around you. Cultivate your curiosity and enthusiasm as you poke around the corners of your world in search of ideas. Reach out and grab the inspirations. Do not sit in your ivory tower waiting for them to come wafting through the narrow slit window on a rare sunbeam. Generally, sources of ideas fall into seven categories:

1. *Yourself.* This includes experiences (past and present, real and imaginary), opinions, hobbies, and special skills, lessons you learn in living and coping and relating to others, things you have already written, jottings in your daily journal, dreams and longings, strong personal interests.

2. *Your family.* Make use of familiar sayings, experiences (both family and individual), hobbies and skills, opinions, problems, heirlooms, and bits of colorful ancestral history, examples of solving relationship problems.

3. *Your friends.* Look at their experiences, hobbies and skills, unusual ministries, distinctive points of view, bits of advice.

4. *Your church.* Here you will find a wide and rich source of ideas in people, activities, programs, projects, special emphases, workable methods, sermons, attitudes.

5. *Your community.* Here is a rich source of people, industries, public services, institutions, historical events or places, organizations, social programs, landmarks or experimental ventures of various sorts.

6. *The media* (newspapers, TV, radio, magazines). Essays, stories of people doing interesting things, or having un-

usual experiences, interesting but little-known facts, editorials, letters to editors, pictures, ads, classified ads (especially the personals)—all hold potential writing subjects for you to investigate and/or to take off with.

7. *Miscellaneous sources.* Telephone directories, books you read, conversations you overhear or take part in, letters, Bible reading, vacations, travel, government publications, club and association meetings, conferences, seminars, words and phrases, movies and plays, health concerns, observed problems, scientific discoveries, technological developments, current issues of social concern, interesting people you meet, gardening and home care, the contents of your purse notebook, recipes, questions that pop into your mind. The more you observe life and write about it, the longer your own personal list of idea sources will grow.

DETERMINING THE WORTH OF AN IDEA

If an idea is going to reach out and grab an editor and later keep a reader glued to the page, it must first pass the following tests:

1. *It must be interesting.* It has to matter terribly or entertain irresistibly. Are you excited about it? If not, do not expect to sell an editor or his readers on it.

2. *It must be significant.* Significance is determined by the audience you aim for and what you intend to do for that audience. Are you attempting to entertain? Inspire? Inform? Whatever your goal, make your reader feel his time was well spent reading your material. He will not forgive you if you cheat him out of his valuable time by giving him trivia.

3. *It must meet needs, answer questions, or deal with problems.* Readers have physical, psychological, emotional, spiritual, intellectual, and social needs. Study people to find out what these needs are; then write with them in mind. If you deal with problems, make something happen and always offer hope.

4. *It needs a universal appeal.* Is your idea so unique that no one else will care about it? The appeal need not be universal to the whole human race, but at least to the readership that you will be asking to read it. Can your target reader see himself in your story? Can he feel with you and welcome your suggestions?

5. *It must offer a fresh new angle.* Centuries ago Solomon said that "there is no new thing under the sun"[5] *(KJV).* But some subjects are overworked, or the approach to them is overworked. Continuing to deal with a universally significant idea demands that you find some compelling new angle.
Example: A much-written-about theme is *Bible study.*

> *Overworked approach:* How to Study Your Bible
> *Better:* Bible Study for Busy People
> How to Get the Bible to Talk to Me
> Motivating Teens to Study the Bible

6. *It must still be timely by the time it reaches the readers.* Learn to think ahead. Allow at least one year of "lead time" when considering magazine ideas. In the case of a book, plan for five or ten years. Learn to read the times and spot the trends, to anticipate what will be "hot" down the line. Only a keen observer living on the cutting edge of life will be able to produce timely stories, articles, poems, books, and dramas.

7. *It must fit the magazine for which you want to write.* Do not send your "Tribute to Mother" to the *Christian Athlete*—unless your mother was an outstanding athlete or you slant your tribute in an athletic direction.

8. *It must be realistic.* Present an accurate, though positive, picture of life. Do not submit untested theories. Admit your own failures and weaknesses; show growth and learning in your own life.

9. *Make sure this idea is within your reach and you can handle it.* Begin by writing the things you know best. Later you can

research and write on the things you do not yet know. When you consider a project that will take a great deal of research, make sure that such research is realistic for you. If the idea proves to be too much for you, leave it for someone else and go on to something you can manage.

FOCUSING IDEAS

To focus an idea means to break it down in such a way that you can give the reader what he wants in the way he wants it and in a size chunk that he can assimilate.

Learn to use the Zoom Lens Technique—changing your writing focus from:

1. *Broad to Narrow.* Avoid big all-inclusive topics that can never be treated with any degree of significance in less than an encyclopedia. Break a big subject into its components; then choose which component you want to work with. Example:

   Too broad: Christian Education
   Better: Junior Church
   Still better: How to start a junior church program that does more than entertain

2. *General to Specific.* Avoid rambling in many directions and saying many words, while in the end communicating nothing beyond vague generalities and ho-hummish impressions. Remember that your readers' needs are specific. Give them specific answers, painted in specific pictures. Example:

   General writing: I'll never forget how much I loved trains when I was a girl. Every new invention in railroads made a lasting impression on me. To this day, I still believe trains are my favorite form of transportation.

   Specific writing: The night was dark. Whether it was cold or hot, wet or dry, I've forgotten. I do remember our whole family stood on the sloping grade of the railroad crossing—waiting.

"I hear the whistle!" my brother shouted.

Seconds later the bright crossing lights flashed red and the bells began to ring. That was a great moment for me—one I would never forget. I was watching and hearing my first electric train signal and I was mesmerized.

3. *Vague to Sharp.* Avoid cluttering your writing with facts and ideas (no matter how fascinating to you) that detract from your main point. Be selective. Stick to those details that build and emphasize your point and further your story.
Example:

Vague: As a teenager, I learned to keep a journal—a daily record of my relationship with God. But later, with the arrival of three babies in three years, the progress of my journal slowed to a near stop. During those years my husband was in the Air Force and we moved a great deal. We lived in thirteen houses in the first ten years of my motherhood. These were scattered all over the United States and Europe. It was a fascinating time of life, and I had many experiences and ideas that would have made excellent journal recordings.

Sharp: As a teenager, I learned to keep a journal—a daily record of my relationship with God. But later, with the arrival of three babies in three years, the progress of my journal slowed to a near stop. For some time, only a few isolated notations of Bible study impressions appeared on its pages.

4. *Distant to Close-up.* Go from impersonal to personal. Be warm and colorful. Admit your failures and slowness to learn; do not preach. Help your reader to identify with you, care about you, and thank you for sharing a bit of yourself with him.
Example:

Distant: If you are like most people, you will always be tempted to do more than you can. When that temptation comes, remember what experience has taught you and follow these logical guidelines for emotional survival.

Close-up: "Two years later, new pressure situations still tempt me to do more than I can, but my keen memories help me to keep things in order. In the process, I have developed what I call my 'Guidelines for Emotional Survival.' They could be helpful to others."[6]

SPECIFIC STEPS IN FOCUSING AN IDEA
(See the following Idea-Focusing Worksheet)

1. Decide on a general subject.

2. Narrow it down to a specific subject.

3. Ask six questions:
    a. What do I want to say? (Theme)
    b. Why do I want to say it? (Significance)
    c. To whom do I want to say it? (Audience)
    d. Where do I want to say it? (Market)
    e. When do I want to say it? (Timing)
    f. How do I want to say it? (Structure and fresh angle)

4. In one sentence summarize the single message you want to share.

[1] Paul Tournier, *The Seasons of Life* (Atlanta: John Knox Press, 1963), p. 43.

[2] Madeleine L'Engle, *A Circle of Quiet* (New York: Farrar, Straus & Giroux Inc., 1972), pp. 217, 218.

[3] Johann Wolfgang von Goethe, *Faustus, A Dramatic Mystery: Prelude at the Theater, Part 1.* trans. John Anster (no publisher given, 1835), p. 303.

[4] From page 6 of *Chosen Families of the Bible* by Ethel L. Herr. Copyright 1981. Moody Press, Moody Bible Institute of Chicago. Used by permission.

[5] Ecclesiastes 1:9.

[6] Ethel Herr, "Slow Down and Live," pp. 18, 28.

IDEA-FOCUSING WORKSHEET_____
Sample

Let God Push George_____
(Working Title)

1. GENERAL SUBJECT: Church Lay Workers
2. SPECIFIC SUBJECT: How to recruit volunteers to do church work
3. WHAT DO I WANT TO SAY? (THEME)

    Recruiting workers need not be a headache, if we learn to let God be our Chief Recruiting Officer.
4. WHY DO I WANT TO SAY IT? (SIGNIFICANCE)

    Most people don't know how to rely on God to help them recruit church lay workers. As a result many people end up doing jobs for all the wrong reasons and often without qualifications.
5. TO WHOM DO I WANT TO SAY IT? (AUDIENCE)

    Church leaders
6. WHERE DO I WANT TO SAY IT? (MARKET)

    Christian education magazine such as *Success*
7. WHEN DO I WANT TO SAY IT? (TIMING)

    Now (If this were a seasonal article, I would plan to send it to my first targeted editor nine to twelve months ahead of the appropriate season.)
8. HOW DO I WANT TO SAY IT? (STRUCTURE AND FRESH ANGLE)

    Article form with introductory anecdote, list of suggested guidelines, and anecdotal illustrations throughout.
9. SUMMARY THEME SENTENCE (MESSAGE):

    God reserves for himself the right to push his people into service. Our part is to inform, inspire, present opportunities, then wait and pray.

ASSIGNMENT:

1. Make a list of at least three ideas you would possibly like to write about. These should be taken from experiences and knowledge you already have.

2. Using the following Idea Evaluation Worksheet for each of your ideas, decide which ones are valid. Choose one that you can write in no more than 1,000 words.
3. Using the Idea-Focusing Worksheet, focus your chosen idea.

IDEA EVALUATION WORKSHEET_____

1. Are you excited about it?
2. Is it sufficiently interesting and significant to keep the reader glued and free from the distraction of more attractive articles?
3. Does it meet needs, answer questions, deal with problems, or provide tools for dealing with issues?
4. Does it have a universal appeal, at least to my target audience?
5. Does it offer a fresh new angle?
6. Is it timely? Will it still be timely by the time it reaches the readers?
7. Does it fit the magazine I am shooting for?
8. Is it realistic?
9. Is the idea within my reach? Can I handle it? Do I know where to go to find material I will need?

If you have answered no to any of these questions, your idea is probably too weak to make it in its present form. Consider some alterations and run the revised idea through the evaluation tests. If nothing works out, then scratch the idea and try another.

IDEA-FOCUSING WORKSHEET_____

_____
(Working Title)

1. GENERAL SUBJECT:

2. SPECIFIC SUBJECT:

3. WHAT DO I WANT TO SAY? (THEME)

4. WHY DO I WANT TO SAY IT? (SIGNIFICANCE)

5. TO WHOM DO I WANT TO SAY IT? (AUDIENCE)

6. WHERE DO I WANT TO SAY IT? (MARKET)

7. WHEN DO I WANT TO SAY IT? (TIMING)

8. HOW DO I WANT TO SAY IT? (STRUCTURE AND FRESH ANGLE)

9. SUMMARY THEME SENTENCE (MESSAGE):

Lesson Six
Part One
How Do I Plan My Work Area and Equipment?

"If only I had a place I could call my office, then I know I could begin to write in earnest."

How many times I have heard these words. Every time someone offers this explanation to me, I recall a series of mental images collected through the years of my associations with writers and professing writers of various kinds. I picture a roomy, well-equipped office filled with just the right equipment and overflowing with books and magazines. It was a writer's dream room! But for several years its occupant used it very little, while she battled with a persistent priority problem.

I remember, too, the living room of another friend. In one corner stood a large card table laden with miniature cardboard file boxes, folders, papers strewn here and there around a typewriter, always with a sheet of paper in it. The person who called this an office could never pass through her living room without a reminder that she was a writer. Consistently it called her to work.

My memory takes me back to another dining room table, situated successively in at least four different houses and always cluttered with papers and books and an old manual

portable typewriter. That was my table, those were my library
books, that was my mess. I had to clean it up every time I prepared a meal for my family. And before my husband returned
from work, I stashed away all the evidence of my relentless
labors so he would be greeted by a calm and orderly house at
the end of a hard day. On this table and under these circumstances, all my articles and poems of several years were born.
My first book was written at this table.

These images have convinced me that a work area neither
makes nor destroys a writer. If you want to write badly enough
so that you cannot stop yourself, nothing else will stop you
either—certainly not the lack of a proper work area. You will
find yourself scribbling notes on bits of wrinkled paper, in
plain notebooks or on church bulletin covers, at kitchen
counters, in the back seat of taxicabs, as you stand in line at
the bank, while lying propped up in bed in the middle of the
night or following a severe illness. In short, if you are a writer,
you will write.

However, one of the greatest aids to a consistent, disciplined program of productive writing is a regular place reserved just for your special activity. Regardless of whether it
is a spacious room, one side of the bedroom, an isolated attic
cubicle, or a tiny corner of the family rumpus room, set aside
for yourself some special place and hang at least a mental
shingle over it that says: WRITER AT WORK.

How large or how isolated the space should be depends on
you and your circumstances. If you are easily distracted by life
around you, a solitary spot is preferable. It may not be possible, however. So you do second best. You plan to write when
the spot is deserted, or you work out a plan to improve your
powers of concentration. Most people feel the ideal is a
quaint, remote seaside cottage or a dusty attic with a grimy
window overlooking some lush garden. These may or may not
be ideal, but they are generally out of our reach. It helps to
remember that idyllic settings can play tricks on a fertile mind
and keep us from concentrating on the thing we are there to
do. Reminding myself of this has often rescued me from the
unproductive rationalization games that frequently seek to
keep me from my typewriter, wherever its home may be for
the present.

Survey your situation, assessing your family needs. Then pick the place that best suits your needs and circumstances. Set up your equipment and leave it there, if possible. If not, find a neat way to store the typewriter, file boxes, and stack of research and reference books for easy recall during your office hours. Ask for your family's understanding indulgence, but do not push them out of shape in some foolhardy attempt to put your writing absolutely first, above them.

Once you have found a work area that is comfortable and well lighted, what equipment do you need in order to begin? Technically, all you need is a pencil, a pencil sharpener (or a paring knife), and some sheets of scratch paper. If this is all you can collect, then go ahead and get started. As you progress, other things can be added.

Typewriter. To type or to write longhand? This question has been batted around among writers since typewriters became a viable option. When I studied my first course in writing, I was told that the professional way to write was to use the typewriter—even for the roughest of rough drafts. I owned a typewriter and knew how to use it. So I tried what I was told and learned that typing works wonders. One of the greatest frustrations of a rough-draft writer is the inability to write fast enough to keep up with the flow of mental images and words. Typing helps to alleviate that, to a certain extent.

I have since learned, however, that a great many world-famous writers (such as C. S. Lewis) never touch or touched a typewriter. Many writers resort to the typewriter only when preparing a final manuscript for submission. Some, especially writers of fiction and poetry, feel that creativity is stifled by the mechanical keys of a typewriter. That is a matter of opinion which may or may not be influenced by planned mental conditioning. Personally, I have a strong dislike for machinery of all kinds. Yet, I have discovered in the typewriter an intimate friend whose services I would never dismiss.

If a typewriter is to serve you well, it needs to be in good condition. Electric or manual? That is up to you. For years I fought the idea of an electric typewriter. It seemed so much more mechanical; a manual typewriter felt closer to the creative pencil. Yet the day came when I tired of sore fingers from

112

typing lengthy book manuscripts. I borrowed a friend's electric machine to type one book manuscript. Promptly I bought an electric machine for myself.

Paper. For rough drafting, you will not need any special kind of paper. Make sure your sheets are uniform in size and that you write on one side only. Discarded sheets of paper still clean on one side make excellent rough draft stock. My husband brings me stacks of such paper from his work. Other friends have other sources—copy stores, stationers, schoolteachers, and the like. I have even resorted to salvaging valuable paper from school trash cans, and I always save blank-sided junk mail letters.

For typing a final manuscript, be choosy. You want neither secondhand paper nor cheap typing paper purchased from the corner dime store. Buy good bond paper—preferably twenty-pound weight. NEVER use corrasable paper. Editors dislike it intensely because it smears and is hard to photocopy.

File boxes. If you can afford metal file cabinets, great—provided you have room to store them. Probably in the beginning you will need to settle for something a bit less expensive. For years I used a couple of cardboard file boxes for my writing needs. I have friends who use regular corrugated cardboard cartons of the right sizes. For your files, you will also need folders and perhaps dividers. Card files and cards will also be valuable to you. (See Appendix 7 for help with filing systems.)

Envelopes. For mailing manuscripts, you will need sturdy manila envelopes. Ideally, they should be in two sizes—9″ x 12″ and 11″ x 14″. When you submit your materials, you will always need to include a SASE (self-addressed stamped envelope). So if you use two sizes, one can fit inside the other quite conveniently. Lacking this convenience, you can always fold the SASE in half.

Desk and chair. I have already alluded to a couple of adequate substitutes for a real desk—dining room tables and card tables. Any sort of table will do as long as it is the right height so you can sit comfortably with your feet resting on the floor. It helps to have a table large enough to accommodate the stack of books and papers you are working with. A separate typewriter table helps as well.

Many writers have developed ingenious makeshift tables, which work well for them—doors mounted on two-drawer filing cabinets, ironing boards, and the like. My husband built my first desk from old moving crates, and it served as a marvelous transition from the dining room table to the real desk I later purchased with my earnings. Make sure the chair you use fits your body, allows you to plant your feet on the floor, and is firm enough to keep you alert.

Miscellaneous supplies. Keep a ready stock of pencils, pens, erasers, paper clips, cellophane tape, scissors, staples, correction fluid or paper, ruler, glue, postage scale, and stamps.

Finally, you will need a writer's reference library. Before you panic, let me explain that your library will, no doubt, begin small and you will add to it gradually. When I began to write, I had five books in my reference library—*Webster's Collegiate Dictionary, Roget's Thesaurus of Words and Phrases, Preparing the Manuscript, Strong's Exhaustive Concordance of the Bible,* and Halley's *Bible Handbook.* I still consider these kinds of books essential, though you might choose different titles. A list of suggested reference materials in several categories—Essential, Great-To-Have, and Specialized Books—is found on pages 237—238.

Every writer needs a dictionary to help with word meanings, spellings, and usage. Also you will need a synonym dictionary to help you expand your vocabulary and enliven your writing. A manuscript preparation guide enables you to answer all those nasty questions about how to prepare a professional manuscript. A writer's market guide is an invaluable tool to help you place your manuscripts where they can minister to people's needs. Bible concordances, dictionaries, commentaries, and handbooks will aid you in making your manuscripts biblically sound and accurate.

Two other little books I have now included on the Essentials list are Jan Venolia's *Write Right* and Flesch and Lass' *A New Guide to Better Writing.* I further recommend a subscription to *The Writer,* America's number-one magazine dedicated to inspiring the production of top-quality writing.

In addition, every writer can use a variety of specialized books to help with specific areas of writing (See the book list in Lesson 4, Part 1).

Finally, if you have an area of expertise that provides you with ideas on which to write, keep a special shelf for research and resource books. I have a shelf on parenting, another on Bible study methods, another on education, and others on topics that I am working on just now.

Having a work area and the right equipment is extremely important to the success of your writing ministry. If God has called you to write, no matter how unpromising your circumstances may look, you can join the company of thousands of other "called" writers and find a place, gather some tools, and go to work without any further delays.

Lesson Six
Part Two
Writing the Personal Experience Story

In Lesson 5 (Part 2), I asked you to reach into your life and pull out three experiences that you have had that would be valuable to share with a reading audience. In this lesson, we will examine the big picture of writing personal experience stories and help you to prepare to write about one of the experiences you have already chosen.

THE RATIONALE FOR BEGINNING
WITH THE PERSONAL EXPERIENCE STORY

1. It allows you to begin with what you already know and involves little or no research.
2. It teaches you to think through an event and analyze its significance. You will take the raw facts of your story, organize them, decide on a theme, and offer your reader something of value for use in his own life.
3. By teaching you how to tell a story, it gives you a foundation for all future writing ventures. Many Christians want to begin by writing devotionals. Filled with truths God has taught them, they are bursting to spread the light around. Their motive is commendable. However, the typical devotional written by a novice usually consists of a preachy

sermonette, which lacks life, sparkle, and attractiveness. Before a writer is ready to write abstract truth, he needs to learn to tell a story that will illustrate that truth.

DEFINITION OF THE PERSONAL EXPERIENCE STORY

A personal experience story is an account of some real-life happening told in such a way as to convey meaning to life.

There are two kinds of personal experience stories:

1. Dramatic happenings, with a universal appeal. Everybody is interested in an exciting, unusual, adventurous encounter with life.
2. Common happenings told dramatically, with a universal appeal.

USES OF THE PERSONAL EXPERIENCE STORY

Personal experience stories can be put to three uses:

1. Lengthy recounting of a complex story with a plot that develops progressively toward a climax. Such stories demonstrate character growth and learning over an extended period of time. These appear as full-length articles (1500 words and longer) or books.
2. A short, concise story centered around a single incident, with one simple and obvious point. Known as a "filler" (tiny bit of material that fills in any small spaces of a magazine page), it runs in length from one short paragraph to one-thousand or twelve-hundred words.
3. An anecdote, which is a "short account of some interesting or humorous incident."[1] Anecdotes are usually similar to 2. above, except that they appear sandwiched in between other kinds of writing, in an article or book for the purpose of:
   a. Illustrating a point
   b. Livening up an article
   c. Changing the pace of an article
   d. Allowing the reader to breathe
   e. Introducing the subject arrestingly
   f. Injecting a touch of humor
   g. Making a point memorably.

SPECIAL TECHNIQUES IN WRITING
THE PERSONAL EXPERIENCE STORY

1. *Strive to make it special.* No matter how exciting and extra-ordinary the story, if you approach it in a dull, reportorial fashion or if you draw from it some time-worn hackneyed application, it will be too common to gain a respectful hearing. No matter how ordinary your story, if you can give it a unique slant or emphasis, it can be special and make a profound impact on your reader.

2. *Be succinct.* Aim for both brevity and clarity. This demands a delicate balance between two potentially contradictory trends:
   a. *Conciseness.* Express yourself in as few words as possible, stripping the narrative of unnecessary elaborateness.
   b. *Thoroughness.* Take whatever time and space you need to tell the story well and to give it color and emotional impact.

3. *Be honest.* Resist the temptation to pad the facts and/or gloss over or omit shady areas. Do not exalt yourself or set yourself up as the perfect example of truth in action. A good way to handle this is to begin your story at the point where you are facing a problem, making a blunder, or becoming aware of a personal weakness. Then through the story, show how your life was changed and you grew as God, family, and friends helped you learn to cope with the problem, recoup from your error, or overcome your weakness. Remember that your reader cannot identify with, or take advice from, a know-it-all.

4. *Be positive.* Remember you are a dispenser of hope to a desperate world. If you cannot offer at least a hint of a solution, then do not bother to share your problems or frustrations.

5. *Do not preach or moralize.* Avoid such statements as "Now as you can learn from my experience...." Present your story without giving the impression that your experience is

the only normal one for all people in similar circumstances or when facing similar weaknesses. Remember that this is an illustration of truth, not a sermonette.

6. *Show—do not tell.* Roll out the color movie camera and take sensory pictures of sights, sounds, smells, textures, moods, tensions. Use active verbs, clear picture nouns, keen mood perceptions. Bring your reader on location and ensnare him in your story as it happened and as you felt it.

7. *Write both to the head and the heart.* Let your full, complex person come through the words on paper. A logical presentation of facts is simply newspaper journalism, which is not your goal in writing the personal experience story. Rather, you are aiming to involve the total person of your reader. You must interpret and give meaning to life as you share the facts of your story.

8. *Make it sound convincing.* Truth is often unbelievable when presented in its raw form. One of the functions of art is, as you may recall, to make order out of the chaos of real life. An important part of this process is writing your story in such a way that the reader can believe it. Find the factors that make the story real and introduce them to the reader, e.g., the power of God and/or the indomitability of a determined will can make many otherwise incredible stories believable.

9. *Include a strong reader takeaway.* Never leave the reader with the question "So what?" If your story is indeed trivial and has nothing to offer, file it under "Practice Pieces" and go on to something that can help the reader, not simply presume on his time.

10. *Structure the personal experience story as follows:*
    a. Problem (Admit to having one.)
    b. Solution (Show how you learned from it, usually as the result of a struggle.)
    c. Outcome (Show the results of applying the solution.)

11. *Emphasize the theme of your story* by choosing one of the following three methods:
   a. Straight narration: Tell the story and let it stand alone, making sure the theme is inherent in the story. (See "Assignment at Sunset" on page 244.)
   b. Narration plus summary: Tell the story; then add a commentary or a summary of points. (See "Slow Down and Live" on page 246.)
   c. Framed narration: Set your story in a beginning-and-ending frame. This introduces a concept, then tells the story as an illustration either with or without a short application at the end. (See "Rags and a Wordless Prayer" on page 248.)

STEPS IN WRITING THE PERSONAL EXPERIENCE STORY

1. *Find a quiet place.* Spend an hour there writing down all the details you can remember about the personal experience you decide to write. Do not worry about order or accuracy of chronology or facts. Just jot down things as you recall them. Concentrate on sensory data (colors, textures, sounds, smells, bodily sensations), moods, reactions, personalities of people you interact with, Scriptures, dialogue, and the like. Exhaust your memory of the event, down to the most trivial detail.

2. *Read through what you have written.* Then ask yourself, "Do I need to research anything? To verify any facts?"

3. *Plan and do your research.* What facts need to be checked in the library? By telephone? By letter? What persons do I need to talk with? Do I have old letters or journals that will help me clarify the story? Is there someone who can help me with doctrinal or scriptural problems? (For more help with research, see Lesson 7, Part 2.)

4. *Organize and plan your story.* (See Lesson 8, Part 2.)

5. *Write your story.* (See Lessons 9 and 10, Part 2.)

6. *Rewrite and polish your story.* (See Lesson 11, Part 2.)

7. *Submit your story to a publisher.* (See Lesson 11, Part 2.)

ASSIGNMENT:

1. Plan a specific place for your working area and begin to assemble equipment needed.
2. Take the personal experience story idea you have chosen and follow Steps 1 and 2 of the specific procedure in this lesson. Plan Step 3. For Steps 2 and 3, use the following Research Planning Sheet. Remember that with most personal experiences you will need to do very little, if any, research.
3. Study the three personal experience stories ("Assignment at Sunset," "Slow Down and Live," and "Rags and a Wordless Prayer" on pages 248–251). Analyze each story to see whether it used the special techniques listed in this lesson.

[1] *American Heritage Dictionary of the English Language.*

RESEARCH PLANNING SHEET_____

I. What needs researching?
   Facts to be verified:

   Doctrinal points to be checked:

   Scriptures to be checked or used:

II. How the research is to be done.
   Library checking:

   Telephone calls to make:

   Letters to write:

   People to talk to:

   Old letters and journals to check:

   Pastors or other people to help with doctrinal or scriptural issues:

Lesson Seven
Part One
How Do I Choose and Evaluate the Writing Market?

If I write but have no audience, it is therapy. When I share my writings with an audience, it becomes communication. I need to learn to do both and do them well. God designs the therapy at least in part for worship. But if he has led me to a writing ministry, I must find ways to break out of my journal in the prayer closet and reach my audience. The vehicle for turning therapy into ministry is that enormous, sometimes nebulous thing we call "The Market."

The Market is the sum total of all the magazines, newspapers, book publishers, and miscellaneous publishing organs that take my written manuscripts and put them on paper or film or send them across the airwaves to make contact with my audience.

If I am going to make all the necessary connections to enable me to complete these transactions successfully, I will have to do some getting-acquainted legwork. Every consistently publishing writer places a high priority on evaluating the market. The procedure takes time, effort, and concentration. Some novices consider it too tedious and time-consuming to be worthwhile. But any shortcut that omits market analysis turns out to be a short circuit.

Market analysis accomplishes three things for us. Each of

these is far too vital to leave to chance—which is what happens when we write at will and submit at random.

1. *Evaluating the market teaches you what is the best place for your materials.* Do you know what magazines would be interested in each of the following:
   A recipe for a successful marriage
   A personality profile of a retiring missionary
   A 2,000-word fiction adventure story for junior high boys
   A long epic poem
   A stage play script
   A sensitive slant on a controversial issue such as involvement in politics?

   If you do not know the markets, you may easily waste endless time and postage sending your manuscripts to all the wrong places. That is a sure way to discouragement. For this reason, in Lesson 2 (Part 1) you were given the assignment to request sample copies and editorial guidelines from several magazines. By now you should have those materials and be ready to study them.

2. *Evaluating the market enables you to reach your target audience.* No matter how valuable your manuscript, it will never help a soul if the right editor does not see it and so fails to pass it on to his readers.

3. *Evaluating the market helps you to plan your writing.* You have an idea, but are not certain how to develop it. You find the magazine that reaches your target audience. As you study it, you get ideas for word length, format, and other details. That sort of guidance is invaluable in helping you to plan and prepare a winner that will hit the goal you are aiming for.

At this point, you have gathered all the little goodies the postman has brought you—sample copies and editorial guidelines. Eager to get acquainted with your new markets, you open the pages. But what should you look for? Should you judge the quality of the articles? Should you look for something specific or only general impressions?

Evaluation begins with observation. Notice the cover. This is high on reader appeal. What sort of artwork does it use? What kind of colors? What titles? Open the magazine and leaf through it, scanning its contents to ascertain its overall atmosphere. Is the writing scholarly? Technical? Humorous? Inspirational? Informative? How much space is given to advertisements? Are the articles mostly short or long? Does the magazine use poetry and filler materials? Cartoons and puzzles? Fiction? Personal experiences? Devotionals? Is the paper slick, newsprint, or something in between?

When you have gotten an overall impression of the magazine, go back and read it—literally from cover to cover. Read every word—covers, advertisements, titles, articles, poems, fillers. Especially note the editorials and letters to the editors.

As you read, fill in the following two worksheets—Market Analysis Sheet and Market Evaluation Worksheet. These two forms will give you a good picture of three things (1) the nature and personality of the magazine and its editors, (2) the nature and needs of the magazine's readers, (3) types of materials the magazine has used.

In addition, read the editorial guidelines provided by the editor and/or all entries you find in other marketing guides or news items from writers' magazines. Two excellent marketing guides are available. (See the list of reference books in Lesson 6, Part 1.)

Now that you are ready to analyze your markets in detail, how do you use the worksheets?

Begin with the *Market Analysis Sheet* on pages 128 – 132. This will serve as an invaluable reference tool when you want to survey the overall market and its needs, to decide which magazine is right for some idea you are working on. Most information for this chart comes from editorial guidelines, but some can be gleaned from the editorial pages of the magazines themselves.

Information you will need to amass:

NAME OF MAGAZINE. This section is simple enough!

DISTINCTIVE SLANT. What is the special emphasis of this magazine? Artsy, poetic materials? Controversial issues? Family topics? General interest topics? Conservative, liberal, charismatic, or Catholic theological approach? Anything that makes this magazine unique from all the others should be included here.

SPECIFIC CATEGORIES. The following five areas will help you to identify the target audience of the publication. All magazines will fit into at least two of these categories. Check the ones that are appropriate and in some cases fill in specific information.

Gen = General, interdenominational Christian audience

Den = Denominational audience. Record which denomination; e.g., Lutheran, Conservative Baptist, Episcopalian.

Them = Thematic audience. These are the missions, women's, sports, family, Christian ed, and other theme types of publications. Indicate which theme applies to the magazine.

Org = Organization for which this magazine is the official publication; e.g., *Decision* is the magazine of the Billy Graham Evangelistic Association. *Evangelizing Today's Child* is the voice of Child Evangelism Fellowship. Record the name of the organization that applies.

Age = Age group that reads this publication. Indicate what the age grouping is; e.g., A = Adult, YA = Young Adult, HS =High School, C = College, All = All ages. For younger children, indicate ages in years (e.g., 3-5, 10-12, etc.).

MATERIALS PURCHASED. The following six areas indicate the types of materials purchased by each magazine. Again, check the category that fits and add any vital information about specific requirements.

Poe = Poetry. Indicate line limits, payment, type of poetry (e.g., *to 8 lines, pays 10¢/line, no avant garde*).

Fic = Fiction. Indicate word length limits, fiction types, payment rates, special requirements (e.g., children's, no science fiction).

Fil = Fillers. Indicate length, payment, and type of materials (e.g., cartoons, quotes, devotionals, anecdotes).

P. Ex = Personal Experience. Indicate word length, payment, special requirements (e.g., first person only, conversions, no children's stories).

Art = Articles (nonfiction). Record word lengths, payment, types of materials, taboos.

Pho = Photographs. Indicate size, color, or b & w (black and

white), transparencies, whether accepted only with manuscripts or alone.

PAYMENT PROCEDURES/RIGHTS. Business details concerned
with rights and payment.

POA = Pays On Acceptance. Indicates that the magazine
pays for your material when they accept it for publication.

POP = Pays On Publication. Indicates that the magazine
accepts your material, then waits until it is published before they pay you.

1st = Buys First Rights Only. Record "All" if the magazine
buys all rights.

Rep = Reprint Rights. This indicates that the magazine pur-
chases reprint rights to materials that have already been
published in another magazine or book.

S. S. = Simultaneous Submission. Many denominational
magazines will accept a manuscript when you submit it
to them and to other denominational magazines at the
same time.

(*Note:* For more information on rights purchased, see Appendix 2—Glossary of Writer's Terms.)

MISCELLANEOUS COMMENTS. Record such things as how
often the magazine is published, whether they require a
query, how quickly they reply, and any other bit of information you consider vital to help you make intelligent market
choices.

Once you have placed the target publication on the Market
Analysis Sheet, fill out a Market Evaluation Sheet as shown on
page 128 (one for each magazine). I am indebted to Margaret J.
Anderson for assistance in compiling this form. This provides
a profile of the periodical so you can get well acquainted with
it and know better how to write to meet the desires and needs
of its editors and readers.

MARKET ANALYSIS SHEET_____

SPECIFIC CATEGORIES

NAME OF MAGAZINE	DISTINCTIVE SLANT	Gen	Den	Them	Org	Age

MATERIALS PURCHASED						PAYMENT PROCEDURES/RIGHTS					MISC. COMMENTS
Poe	Fic	Fil	P. Ex	Art	Pho	POA	POP	1st	Rep	S. S.	

HOW DO I CHOOSE AND EVALUATE THE WRITING MARKET?

Items 1 — 6: Take this information from the Market Analysis Sheet.

Item 7: Glean this from reading advertisements, letters to the editor, types of articles, general atmosphere of the magazine, editorial remarks, and the magazine section listing editorial facts and policies.

Items 8 — 10: Do not attempt to fill in these until you have studied *leads* (Lesson 9, Part 2), *titles* (Lesson 9, Part 2), and *style* (Lesson 11, Part 2).

Item 11: Ascertain this by reading editorial columns and examining types of materials used in the magazine.

Item 12: Most of this material can be taken from the Market Analysis Sheet. Otherwise, check editorial guidelines and sample copies. Remember that an accurate picture of these items cannot be gained simply from studying one sample copy.

Item 13: Record the special kinds of things you need to remember when working with a particular market. Some magazines refuse to touch controversial issues, most insist on a query, and others prefer personal experience topics.

Item 14: Take this from the Market Analysis Sheet.

Item 15: This is helpful when you need first, second, third, and additional optional markets for submitting a manuscript.

Item 16: This includes miscellaneous observations and personal feelings about the magazine. What is its quality standard? Would you feel comfortable seeing your name in this magazine? Can you identify with its readership? Does its editorial philosophy/doctrinal position pose any threats to you? Would you consider it a top-priority target or a last resort?

If this seems like a lot of work, remember that you will not do it all in a day. And you will not need to suspend all writing until you have completely exhausted your study of the markets. Plan to make market study an ongoing part of your writing ministry.

However, when an idea is burning so intensely in your heart that you are tempted to omit all market analysis and take your chances, resist the temptation. Set the idea on paper, yes. But at the same time, examine the markets, and make the submission process an intelligent one. Along with perpetual observation, develop the habit of constantly looking for and analyzing new markets.

MARKET EVALUATION SHEET _____

1. Name of publication _____
2. Address _____
3. Editor/editors _____
4. Publication frequency _____ Denomination _____
5. Magazine type: General _____ Specialized _____
   Organizational _____ Other _____
6. Slant _____
7. Readership profile: Age _____ Educational level _____
   Occupations _____ Special interests _____
8. Lead types _____
9. Title types _____
10. Style (formal, informal, satirical, etc.) _____
11. Editorial viewpoint and philosophy _____
    _____

12. Materials used:

	No.	Type	Word length	Subject matter	Misc.
Articles					
Fillers					
Fiction					
Columns/ Features					
Poetry					
Puzzles & Quizzes					
Photos					

13. Special requirements _____
14. Rights purchased _____ Payment _____
15. Similar or competitive publications _____
    _____

16. Comments: _____
    _____
    _____
    _____
    _____
    _____

HOW DO I CHOOSE AND EVALUATE THE WRITING MARKET?

Lesson Seven
Part Two
Doing Research

The word *research* draws varied reactions from people. Some love it, flourish on it, would gladly spend their entire lives doing it. Others think of it as a stuffy, lifeless, windowless prison where the mind must grovel through layers of dust in search of a precious few gems.

Regardless of the category you fit into, the word may need some demythologizing. One writer reminds us that "research is, remember, an exchange of ideas."[1] What is common knowledge to you may turn out to be the treasure I need to spark a new idea, to help me fill in some missing pieces in my background knowledge, or to authenticate an opinion.

Doing research does not always mean frequenting musty library shelves to read dry textbooks and collections of ancient documents. Simply, research is the process of gathering materials from a wide variety of sources; its purpose is to enrich your own background on a subject and to lend depth and substance to the things you share with your readers. Depending on the circumstances, your bent, and the difficulty of the project, research can be either great fun or a tedious duty. But whether you call it fun or drudgery, it will always be hard work.

THE BENEFITS OF RESEARCH

1. *Research broadens your background and understanding* of all you plan to write. Virginia Muir, from Tyndale House Publishers, says this about research: Your writing should reflect an immense amount of research background. Write out of an abundance, not poverty of heart and head. Be so full of your subject that what you write is the overflow, not the whole wad.

2. *Research helps you to crystallize your thinking.* Remember that writing is the artistic process of taking a generous supply of life's raw materials and sorting, discarding, rearranging them in such a way that you make order out of the chaos in which we normally experience them. We have to do a lot of living, investigating, and thinking if we are to find this order. Consequently, in most cases, while a writer uses only a small percentage of the actual material he gathers in research, not a scrap of it is wasted.

3. *Research lends authority to what you write.* "Quotes validate your arguments" and "add both charm and substance," writes Marjorie Holmes.[2] A hastily composed piece based solely on personal observation or opinion may give the effect of being flimsy, trite, or shallow.

4. *Research can correct or confirm your assumptions and/or remembered impressions.* It also gives you greater confidence in your approaches and conclusions.

5. *Research helps you to understand your potential readers' objections and/or differences of opinion.*

6. *Research sparks new ideas or fresh angles for future projects.*

THE THREE BASIC KINDS OF RESEARCH

1. *Firsthand Research.* This is information you obtain directly from people, places, or events. You experience it yourself, then report it. It includes such things as:

a. *Interviews,* preferably in person, but also on telephone or by letter or tape recording. (See Appendix 4, pages 272 – 273 for the techniques of interviewing.) Max Gunther says, "It is ten times better to quote what a man has said than what he has written."[3]

b. *Visits to unfamiliar places.* While it is possible to write effectively about a place you have never seen, it is much more difficult to do so convincingly. This category also includes places revisited for the purpose of refreshing the memory.

c. *On-the-spot, eyewitness experiences.* Either your own or someone else's.

d. *Original documents.* Letters, diaries, wills, and other legal papers.

2. *Memory Research.* Call up the slumbering giants in your subconscious and prod them into revealing their secrets. Refer to outdated journals, diaries, scrapbooks, letters, and other pieces of memorabilia. Visit friends or family members and reminisce about days gone by. Such brainstorming is particularly enlightening, because each person will remember an event somewhat differently. As you discover a variety of slants, you will be better able to understand the real truth, by examining each one with care and drawing cautious conclusions.

3. *Printed Page Research.* Here are all those sources we normally classify as research—newspapers, magazines, books, libraries, museums. When considering books, check out the secondhand bookstores, library book sales, garage sales, Goodwill and Salvation Army stores. I have found some valuable gems in these unlikely places.

When you think of libraries, do not stop with the public library in your community. While there, ask for lists of specialized libraries of many sorts—corporate, personal, governmental, university and college, special interest, church and seminary libraries. Many of these, though not located in your community, are valuable sources of mail-order information. Often you can obtain materials from all over the country, through interlibrary loans. Further, museums are excellent sources of both unprinted and printed materials.

Check with your local librarian for the many sources of mail-order research, as well. Government agencies print excellent written material on an unbelievably wide variety of topics. You can find congressional records in your public library or order them through the mail. Industries and organizations are eager to share information with writers, through their PR (Public Relations) departments. Try the denominational headquarters of your church or whatever church can help you with the specific needs of your project.

THE EXTENT OF RESEARCH

How much research should you do? Is it possible to do too much?

1. *Consider the size of your project and its deadline.* A full-length book will demand far more research than a 1500-word article. If a piece is so timely that it must be on an editor's desk within a month, you will obviously not have time to carry on a full-blown research campaign.

2. *Make a list of questions.*
   a. *Factual questions.* Get enough accurate factual information to support whatever you write.
   b. *Motivational questions.* What made him do what he did? How did this organization begin? What caused such a drastic change in this movement? What are the real problems?
   c. *Application questions.* How can all that I have been researching apply to the lives of my readers today—and tomorrow? What parallels can be drawn? What guidelines for life are inherent in this subject?

Begin looking for answers to these questions. Your search will often suggest more questions. When all your questions are either answered or proven to be unanswerable or insignificant, you have probably exhausted your subject.

3. *Research to capture the mood, culture, or circumstances.* Especially with mood pieces, works set in another time or culture, and subjects totally new to you, research until you feel yourself transported into the strange time, culture, mood, or circumstances. Keep at it until you get inside the skin of the persons about whom you are writing.

4. *Discipline yourself to stop researching in time to write.* Many aspiring writers fall in love with the research and develop such a paralyzing fear of missing something vital that they never get around to doing the actual writing. A helpful rule to follow is this bit of advice offered to writers of history:

> "When one comes to the point that his reading, study and thinking are turning up little that is new about his subject, one should start writing. . . ."[4]

DOING THE ACTUAL RESEARCH WORK

1. *Keep your eyes and ears open all the time.* Train your physical and mental antennae to be habitual researchers. Material of value—ideas, facts, names, and leads—appears at the least likely moments and in the least likely places. Much of your most valuable research will be unplanned. Learn to live your project.

2. *Refer to original sources whenever possible.* Do not rely on secondhand analyses of other people's comments or ideas. Do your own thinking and analyzing.
Example:

> When I read and heard that John Dewey advocated humanistic educational methods, I found John Dewey's work and read it for myself.

3. *Read whole works, not just bits and pieces.* This does not mean that you should never read portions of anything. At least read enough so that you get an accurate picture of

138

what is being said and so that you understand the basic philosophy and thesis of the author you are reading. Likewise, do not take a man's speech out of context and thus draw hasty conclusions from a single message.

4. *Let your research suggest new ideas.* Sometimes this will mean changing the direction of your present project. At other times, it will give you ideas for new projects to try later.

5. *Make accurate notes of acknowledgments, bibliographies and the names of people and books quoted.* Follow these up for further information. When I researched my book on parent involvement in education, I found this technique opened up for me an incredible chain of resources, many of them the most valuable I found for the whole project.

6. *Read with an open mind.* Read all sides of an issue. Read about an event from as many viewpoints as are available. Be honest in evaluating what you can find. Reserve judgment until you have gathered all the evidence. This process can be traumatic, but it is the only way to assure objectivity and credibility with your readers. You are not called to perpetuate emotional biases, but to present truth and let it change lives, including your own.

7. *Do not overlook children's books in your research.* Sometimes these are the best sources you will find on a topic. Look at both fiction and nonfiction.

8. *Be sure to read what magazines have to offer on a subject.* Learn to use the *Reader's Guide to Periodical Literature* in your library. Here you will find all the articles published on a given topic during the time covered by the issue of the guide you are looking at. Ask your librarian to help you learn to use it.

9. *Prepare a basic tentative outline before you begin extensive research.* Let it guide you, but be flexible and allow your research to help you reexamine the outline and refine your

piece. Something you plan to cover as a subtopic may not yield enough information to allow you to write about it authoritatively. In the process, you may find some other subtopic which offers more information and/or greater significance. Thus, you should drop the original subtopic and substitute the new one.

10. *Be persistent, but courteous.* Do not become easily discouraged when the information you are searching for seems doggedly determined to evade you. Heed the classical advice of Columbus: "Sail on! Sail on and on!"[5] At the same time be careful not to push other people around or be rude to them as you seek their cooperation and help in obtaining your materials.

11. *Make friends with your local reference librarian.* Librarians love writers and are more than eager to serve you.

RECORDING RESEARCH INFORMATION

1. *Take notes on uniformly sized cards or paper.* This facilitates use and storage of the information.

2. *Limit yourself to one subject or one note per card or page.* Record the subject in the upper righthand corner.

3. *Always record complete bibliographic information.* This includes the author, title, publisher, date, magazine, and site of publication—all placed at the top of the card or sheet of paper before you start making notes. If you slough off here, it can cause you untold grief later on. I know!

4. *When researching from a book, follow a special procedure.*
   a. Study the table of contents and introductory materials in order to determine whether this is indeed something you need. Decide which chapters will be of value to you.
   b. Skim the promising chapters to get an overview and determine whether they carry through on the promises made in the introduction and/or titles. Then go back and

140

read the details to get the information, opinion, or mood you need.

5. *Always make your notes clear and complete.* Do not trust your memory or leave anything for another trip.

6. *Paraphrase some things you read.* Record exact quotes when you feel you will need them to use as quotes or for best understanding of the real meaning. Make sure to enclose quotes in quotation marks so you can later identify them as such.

7. *Develop your own form of shorthand.* This saves time in writing notes. Let it grow gradually and make it neither so spontaneous nor so complicated that you cannot decipher it yourself. Of course, you may already have one.

8. *Focus on the actual subjects you are researching.* Otherwise, you will easily become sidetracked and waste valuable time.

9. *Evaluate the validity of your sources.* Not all sources are equally reliable or accurate. Use discernment. Learn to spot unfairly slanted materials and to distinguish fact from fiction.

10. *Jot down any additional, though unrelated, ideas that suggest themselves.* Then go on. Do not take time to deal with them now. Put them on a separate sheet of paper, being especially careful to note full source details, including where you found the book or magazine.

ASSIGNMENT:

1. Fill in both the Market Analysis Sheet and Market Evaluation Sheet for the sample magazines you have received.
2. Complete the following Library Research Assignment.
3. Using your Research Planning Sheet from Lesson 6, Part 2, do the research planned from Step 3.

[1]Louise Zobel, *The Travel Writer's Handbook* (Cincinnati: Writer's Digest, 1980), p. 10.

[2] Marjorie Holmes, *Writing the Creative Article* (Boston: The Writer, 1973), p. 73.

[3] Max Gunther, *Writing the Modern Magazine Article* (Boston: The Writer, 1973), p. 48.

[4] Cairns, *God and Man in Time*, p. 162.

[5] Joaquin Miller, "Columbus (1492)," edited by Nora Beuft el. al., *American Backgrounds* (E. M. Hale and Company, 1958), pp. 34, 35.

LIBRARY RESEARCH ASSIGNMENT_____

1. Locate the following, and indicate where you found each item:

Telephone directories
California collection
U. S. Agricultural Extension display
Writer's Market
Atlases
Newspapers
Encyclopedias (Reference only)
              (Circulating)
Shelf books on writing techniques
Shelf books on English grammar and usage
Shelf books on biblical backgrounds and commentaries
Shelf books of biographies
Biblical reference books
Almanacs and statistical books
Books of quotations
College directories and catalogs
Vertical file of pamphlets and folders
Reader's Guide to Periodical Literature

2. List the following:

5 special encyclopedias (e.g., art)
5 atlases
5 magazines new to you. List name and subject area.
5 books of quotations
5 kinds of indexes (e.g., education)

3. How did you react to this assignment? Share any new ideas you may have gotten in the process.

Optional Research Assignment
Using the library, find the following information:
1. Search for these facts. Answer each question and list source where you found the answer.

a. List 5 animals that are classified as endangered species.
b. Who holds the world chess championship? What country is he/she from?
c. Find address and name of the editor of *Cat Fancy* magazine. Does this magazine buy poetry? If so, what kind?
d. What is the land area of Kenya? How does this compare to the U. S.? The State of California?
e. How many people compose the President's cabinet?
f. How high is Mt. McKinley?
g. Who invented the tape recorder?

2. Verify the accuracy of the following facts. Again, list source of your information.
a. A woodpecker's diet consists of worms.
b. The largest pyramid in the world is the Great Pyramid of Egypt.
c. Plymouth was the first permanent colony in the U. S., settled by complete families.
d. The Island of Krakatoa is an ecological wonder. All life was destroyed there in 1883 by a volcanic eruption. Less than fifty years later, a full rich jungle covered the island once more. Wind-blown or floating seeds and animals washed ashore on drifting debris apparently restored life to the island.
e. The Mississippi River is the longest in the world.
f. Savonarola, a great Italian Reformer, was martyred in 1598.

3. In a paragraph or two, tell about the way in which people in another culture (modern or historical—you pick it) open their homes to extend hospitality.

4. Find the origins of the following words:
geranium, hermit, heathen, toast, blackmail, Eureka, preposterous

5.
a. Find the following information about John Muir:
Birthdate_____ Birthplace_____
Names of parents_____
Wife_____ Children_____
Brothers and sisters_____
Where he lived most of his life:_____
Various occupations:_____

Outstanding achievements:————————————————
Basic philosophy of life:————————————————
One important or impressive quotation:————————
Where and when did he die?————————————————
Places named for him, as living memorials:————————

   b. Find the same information about C. S. Lewis.

Lesson Eight
Part One
How Do I Structure My Writing?

During the sixties and seventies the counterculture element in our American colleges and universities spawned a popular movement toward unstructured composition. According to their philosophy, anything as creative as writing must never be subjected to rules or forced into a framework. Writing was perceived as a rambling attempt to let their inner persons lounge about on paper. Most fiction stories were left open-ended, with no resolution. Poetry became an exercise in self-expressive therapy. Much of what those confused souls called stories could have been more accurately labeled "stream of consciousness" writing in which the writer sits down to his typewriter and writes everything that comes to mind, just as it comes.

By contrast, God is a God of order, design, and pattern. Nature profusely displays his structure orientation. Certainly none of us can suggest that such structure has stifled his creativity. He who could have done anything in any way he chose planned and created his world by design.

Further, God shared with us, as a part of his image in man, a strong need to live with order, structure, and limits. Hence, when we read aimless essays, poems, and novels, something in us feels empty and dissatisfied. Since structure is such an

146

integral part of us, we might expect it to come easily when we write. That would be wonderful, but it simply does not work that way. Our fallen human natures have turned order into chaos, so that if we would write materials that will meet needs, we must study pattern and work hard to polish our craft.

Before you use the materials you have been gathering in your idea jottings and research, I invite you to look at literary structure, to define it, and to determine how you will handle it on the printed page.

Structure in writing is a planned order of words, ideas, and sentences designed to entice, captivate, and satisfy the reader. You would not think of building a house without a planned frame, consisting of foundation, studs, and roof beams. Nor should you consider writing without the elements that will hold your piece together when you start doing the actual writing.

Good structure consists of three essential elements: unity, coherence, and emphasis. Bergan Evans summarizes the interaction of these principles:

> A *unified* piece involves the consistent fulfillment of a writer's theme and purpose. A *coherent* piece is one in which the relationship between sentences and paragraphs is clear and meaningful. An *emphatic* piece is one which allows your readers to see ideas in the relative importance you intended.[1]

UNITY

Unity is the single significant purpose that holds a piece of writing together. It can be compared to many things—a track for a train to run on, a compass to keep the reader traveling in the right direction, a strong love that motivates action. Often it has been called a Red String.

Well-structured writing contains at least four kinds of unity:

1. *Unity of theme.* Know what you want to say and do not digress. My children once had a charming storybook about a little train engine named Tootle. He went to school to

learn how to become a streamlined engine. Of all the difficult lessons he learned there, one he was told he had to master or he would never graduate. It was simply to "stay on the rails, no matter what."[2] He worked hard and learned well. Then one day he raced a black horse through a pleasant meadow and jumped off the rails to avoid a curve that would have made him lose the race. Here he discovered the most alluring array of buttercups and daisies, birds and butterflies. After that, he was never able to round that curve without hopping off the rails and playing among the buttercups, until local villagers devised a plan to keep him on the rails.

Unity of theme means "staying on the rails," no matter how enticing the buttercups in your literary meadows.

2. *Unity of point of view.* In short pieces, you must always tell your story through the eyes of one person only. Be consistent about which person you use. A frequent mistake of beginning writers is that of starting in one point of view and slipping into another. Writing texts do not agree on point of view categories. For our purposes, with short materials, we will refer to three:

   a. *First-person reporting point of view.* This is *my* story. I tell my audience what I say, do, think, and feel and what happens to me.
   Example:

   > From my chaise lounge on the patio, I heard the telephone ring.

   b. *Third-person reporting point of view.* This is *his* or *her* story. I tell you what he or she says, does, thinks, and feels and what happens to him or her.
   Example:

   > From her chaise lounge on the patio, she heard the telephone ring.

   c. *First-person intimate point of view.* Here is where *I* the writer chat with *you* the reader. Louise Boggess, in her book *Writing Articles That Sell,* calls this the I-You Viewpoint. It can be accomplished by using both *I* and *you.*

Example:

> *I'd* like to suggest steps *you* can take that will help *you* to master the art of gracious receivership.

More often, you will substitute the word *we* for *you*. It is less threatening to a reader who may resent being told what to do.
Example:

> I'd like to suggest steps *we* can take that will help *us* to master the art of gracious receivership.

Note: Several other kinds of points of view used are in longer works, but we shall not discuss them here.

3. *Unity of tense.* Either tell a story all in the *past* tense (He munched on his mother's cookies all the way to the station) or the *present* tense (He munches on his mother's cookies all the way to the station). Do not mix tenses. Most beginners do. With a little conscious effort you can learn to be consistent.

4. *Unity of mood.* If you intend to be humorous, do not start out in a scholarly mood. If you aim to be inspirational, do not scold your reader with a moralizing conclusion. If your mood is devotional, do not include satire.

All the moods have their place. But if you mix them they will cancel each other out, ruin the unity of your piece, and confuse the reader. This does not mean that you can never use humor in a serious piece. Quite the contrary is true. The more ponderous subjects often need the lightening effect of tiny touches of humor. In the process, however, do not poke fun at things or people that should not be poked fun at. Be sparing with your joviality. Use it when it serves your purpose and fits into your careful design for effect and emphasis.

COHERENCE

Coherence is the smooth flow of an article or story that allows you to read it without stumbling over thoughts, words, and awkward constructions. Our goal here is to provide clear understanding at a single reading—not necessarily complete appreciation of the full depth of a piece, but at least clarity. Unless we are specifically writing puzzles, we should not be offering our readers any mysterious packages.

Coherence is achieved in two ways:

(1) *By the use of transitions.* Transitions are usually single sentences, words, or phrases, but may be whole paragraphs or scenes. They tie two thoughts together so that the reader can see a clear relationship between them. Examples: Connective words and phrases such as *further, in the same way, two years later, however, such as, consequently.*

(2) *By developing the theme logically.* Each sentence should appear to grow out of the one before it. Ideas should lead naturally from one to the next. Start with simple points and go on to the more complex ideas. You may state your thesis and then support it with evidences, component ideas, and illustrations and end by summarizing the theme in different words. You may introduce a story with a scene taken from the middle of a sequence of events. Or you may present a flashback to something in the past that gives meaning to your story. However, you will generally tell a story in clear chronological order so the reader does not get lost. Whatever your technique, plan the order of thoughts and sentences so as to show growth, development of thought, progress toward some goal—all in a believable sequence.

EMPHASIS

Emphasis is the proper attention to words, thoughts, and parts of a piece so they stand out and assume their intended significance. It means making ideas, persons, places, and things memorable.

Most beginning writers attempt to emphasize points by using one or all of the following faulty methods. Don't imitate them, but instead

1. *Avoid wordy expansion of a thought.* The theory here is that if I want you to get my point, I clobber you with it. True, we do need to devote more wordage to a key thought than to

some insignificant supporting idea. However, excessive wordiness actually has the effect of minimizing effectiveness.

2. *Avoid mechanical techniques.* Many writers pepper their manuscripts with exclamation marks, dashes, italics, capital letters, and other such devices. At times, and in moderation, these tools are helpful, but they must be used sparingly and only when nothing else will do the trick. Learn to make your word choices and arrangements do the work with a minimum of assistance from mechanical crutches.

3. *Preachiness.* If you want somebody to know some great eternal truth, you preach at him, right?

Wrong. Preaching shouts messages. Writing shares insights into truth. The most effective stories are those that do their sharing silently, as a part of the story itself, not through a moral tacked onto the end.

TEN TOOLS TO INCREASE EMPHASIS

You can avoid the above three faulty methods by mastering the use of ten technical tools for increasing emphasis. Rarely will you use all ten in any one piece, but you do need to become proficient in their use.

1. *Poignant statement.* Keep it brief, fresh, provocative. The truth may not be unusual or revolutionary. Your reader may have agreed with you all his life. Strive to say it with such punch that he will never forget it.

2. *Proper arrangement of words, sentences, and ideas.* In the beginning parts of sentences, paragraphs, and sections, emphasize those things that can arrest the reader's attention and prepare him for the meat of your unit of thought. End with something that either satisfies the reader or leads him on to your next sentence, paragraph, or section.

"Emphasis . . . means ending each statement of a thought —each paragraph, each section, each chapter—with a good, solid, final thump."[3]

3. *Colorful style.* Show rather than tell. Paint vivid pictures, reproduce memorable experiences, make your writing seem believable.

4. *Element of surprise.* Nothing delights a reader like a surprise ending, a turn of events, or a lesson learned. Nor does any idea stay with him longer.

5. *Sharp focus.* "Stay on the rails, no matter what." Meandering in the buttercups confuses the reader and gives him false signals about what you are trying to say.

6. *Quotes and dialogue.* Quotation marks increase readability. Quote a well-known person and your whole piece becomes more authoritative. Use some dialogue and you bring your reader on location by letting him hear it for himself.

7. *Anecdotes.* Short stories with a strong point liven up an article and sometimes even a longer story. We all remember stories longer than theoretical points in an outline. Make sure the anecdote is a solid illustration of the thing you are trying to say, and it will do wonders for your emphasis.

8. *Repetition.* Prudent use of this tool makes for a strong emphasis. Use it to create and preserve a mood. It also works well to use an incident or idea in your beginning and then to come back to it in your conclusion. Repetition is particularly important in scripts that are to be heard by an audience rather than read (i.e., radio, TV, drama).

9. *Plot.* This word is normally thought of as a fictional story line created in the writer's mind. However, more correctly, it refers to the structure of storytelling which introduces a problem, builds up to a climactic point through conflict, then resolves the problem. Proper ordering of plot is essential in putting emphasis where you want it in order to communicate a thesis through your story (See Fiction Plot Plan chart in Lesson 9, Part 2).

10. *Lead your reader to discovery.* I once heard that everybody wants to learn, but nobody wants to be taught. We learn

better by experience than by lecture. Hence, anything a writer can do to coax his readers into having an experience for themselves will make the truth more emphatic.

Learning to write with effective structure begins by reading well-structured writing. Develop the habit now of reading widely with an eye on the three elements of structure—unity, coherence, emphasis. Analyze all you read with the Structural Analysis Worksheet on page 162. After a while, it will become second nature for you to look for themes, points of view, transitions, logical developments, and emphatic techniques.

Lesson Eight
Part Two
Organizing the Story

In Part 2 of Lessons 6 and 7 you chose a personal experience to share in 1,000 words or less. You also jotted down in rough form all the facts and ideas you could recall related to that experience. Next you planned and collected outside research information needed to make the story authentic and complete. Finally, you studied market possibilities and chose a target publication for your story.

You now have a notebook filled with random ideas, word pictures, facts, perhaps even some quotes and interesting descriptions of people, places, or events.

What next? How do you turn this precious raw material into a sharp little story that your chosen editor will snap up in a hurry? In this lesson, we will look at the three steps to organizing your material so you can begin to write.

SLANTING THE MATERIAL

A *slant* is an approach to a story that makes it meaningful to a specific reader. Recalling the three elements of structure, read through your jottings and look for a key or a theme that will draw the facts together and give you a slant.

There are two methods of slanting. One is the *shotgun*

method in which you tell the story with no thought for theme, idea, or emphasis. Here you spread your ammunition in a general direction, hoping it will hit a target, somehow, somewhere. The second method is the *pistol method* in which you aim carefully at a specific spot and deliver your theme-oriented story with precision. Obviously the second method is the only one worth your efforts.

HOW TO PLAN YOUR SLANT

1. *Know your material.* Are there vital questions still unanswered? Then go after them. If they are unattainable and the story depends on them, then you must either (a) scrap the project, (b) shelve the project until a later time when you may find the answers, or (c) find some other angle by which you can avoid the missing material and still have a valid story.

   Are problems with interpreting the story still unresolved in your mind or heart? Often the process of analyzing the story will give you the resolutions you need. If this fails, then let the story lie until you can deal with it.

2. *Know your theme.* What one thing are you trying to tell your readers? State it in a *single simple sentence.* Your theme may fall in one of the following categories. Study the samples.
   a. *Question theme:*
      Do family holiday celebrations have any spiritual value?
   b. *Set-of-facts theme:*
      Ten things my child needs to know before he starts school.
   c. *Adventure theme:*
      How God protected us in an avalanche.
   d. *Problem theme:*
      How I learned to survive the morning rush to get my family out of the house.
   e. *Place theme:*
      A visit to a tiny church in Spain taught me to value my freedom of worship.

f. *Inspirational/moral theme:*
> How a vacation taught me to relax and apply the therapy of God's handiwork to jangled nerves.

g. *Biographical vignette theme:*
> What I learned about the peace of God from watching a friend die of cancer.

h. *Personal opinion theme:*
> Why I believe in strict home discipline.

i. *Doctrinal theme:*
> An experience that taught me the true meaning of God's justice.

3. *Know your purpose.* What are you trying to do for your reader? All writing is done for at least one of four reasons:
   a. *To entertain:* amuses, pleases, makes reading enjoyable, interests, tantalizes, excites, engages reader's attention
   b. *To inform:* educates, shares facts and opinions, reveals
   c. *To stimulate:* arouses the reader to think or feel something, either in agreement or disagreement with you
   d. *To persuade:* changes the reader's mind and arouses him to action

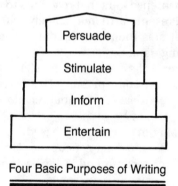

Four Basic Purposes of Writing

These four purposes build on one another (See diagram). In order to inform a reader, you must first get his attention (usually by entertaining him). You cannot stimulate him to think or to feel without informing him. Certainly you cannot persuade a reader without stimulating him.

156

4. *Know your market.* Here is where all that time-consuming market analysis pays off. It tells you how to slant your material and aim with pistol precision to reach your target audience.

CHOOSING A LITERARY FORM

Will you write your story as a poem, an anecdote, an inspirational article, or what?

1. *Learn about the forms.* The forms are almost limitless. Here are the familiar ones from which to choose:
    a. *Prayer:* Opens your heart to God on paper so the reader learns by listening in.
    b. *Poem:* Gives the germ of an experience and some observation made or lesson learned from that experience. Usually short and limited to one sharp emotional idea.
    c. *Narrative:* Tells a story chronologically, either with or without interpretive comments called "frames."
    d. *Journalized story:* Tells a story chronologically, using dates, as if it were recorded in a journal. Usually includes intense personal reactions to events.
    e. *Article:* Presents a theme, usually with a set of points and illustrates them with quotes, anecdotes, statistics, supporting data.
    f. *Open letter:* Tells a story as if in a letter to a friend, organization, or public person. This form allows you to inject a great deal of personal reaction and interpretation.
    g. *Fiction:* May or may not be based on personal experiences. Uses imaginary people, places, and circumstances. Not recommended for beginners as a method for sharing true-life experiences.
    h. *Essay:* Takes a personal story and makes it the basis for an expression of opinion about some matter of vital importance to the reader.
    i. *Nostalgic memoir:* Recounts some past event or lesson learned, emphasizing the value of reflection on a colorful past as a positive means to provide uplift for the present and future.

j. *Travelogue:* Tells the story of some trip you took. A dangerous form for beginners, for unless done extremely well, it will bore everyone but the author. Successful travelogues have unusually significant and interesting angles and adhere tightly to their themes.

k. *Vignette or character sketch:* Tells a story of another person as seen through your eyes, showing admirable qualities or important lessons you learned from him/her.

l. *How-to:* Shares the step-by-step process by which you accomplished some feat of importance to a reader.

m. *Exposé:* Points up a problem of a universal nature and suggests some realistic way to work toward its solution.

n. *Full-length book:* Gives the depth your story may demand. Do not attempt this as your first project. Pick a smaller story and practice your craft before you launch into a book.

Experiment with the forms. Do not write off any form as impossible before you have given it several honest tries. You will never know what you can do unless you experiment.

OUTLINING YOUR STORY

1. *Consider the outline.* Here are four good reasons to use one:
   a. It helps you to develop your ideas in logical sequence.
   b. It helps you to achieve unity, coherence, and emphasis, because it allows you to see an overview of your piece before you write it.
   c. It helps you to spot and correct many structural difficulties, such as roaming among the buttercups.
   d. It helps to provide continuing momentum for the writing process. A completed outline guides you on from one point to another and prevents many mental blocks between points.

2. *Know the kinds of outlines available.*
   a. *Point outline* (used mostly for articles)

158

Consists of:
1) Introduction
2) Body of the article (points)
3) Conclusion
   b. *Chronological outline.* Lists events in sequence as they happened.
   c. *Chronological-in-a-frame outline.* A *frame* is a point of contact which makes the telling of your story meaningful to your reader.
      Opening frames may consist of:
         A theme statement
         A question related to the theme
         One event in your story lifted out of sequence to get attention, because it points directly to your story problem
         A startling statement related to the theme.
      Closing frames may consist of:
         A theme statement
         A summary
         Application questions or challenges.

3. *Make an outline.*
   a. Collect your materials—sheets of paper or index file cards. Bring together in one place, usually in a file folder marked with some sort of working title for your story.
   b. Sort your materials
      1) Read through all your notes.
      2) Jot down different points, idea categories, or events in sequence.
      2) Search for possibilities for an attention-getting opening that will give a clue to your theme (See Lesson 9, Part 2).
      4) Put your points in order. Shuffle them around, if need be, until they fit together logically. Eliminate unnecessary points and ideas, and save them for use in another story. Limit your number of points in an article (3-5).
   c. Make a simple skeleton outline with notations of sources, quotes, and anecdotes. An alternative is to make an outline complete with all your subpoints, perhaps

even written in sentence form. I personally have difficulty with this kind of outline, but it may help you.

d. Some accomplished authors do most of the outlining in their heads. *Do not try this while you are learning basic steps.* Learn to live by the rules before you try to break them!

The following pages contain a sample outlining procedure for "Slow Down and Live" on page 246.

[1] Bergen Evans, *Famous Writers Course*, 1969, Vol. 1, p. 190.

[2] Gertrude Crampton, *Tootle* (Racine WI; Golden Press, 1945).

[3] Max Gunther, *Writing and Selling a Non-Fiction Book*, p. 74.

SLANT WORKSHEET _____

1. Subject: Time and energy management.
2. Theme: If you want to survive emotionally in today's society, you have to learn to slow down and enjoy living.
3. Purpose: To inspire readers to take life at a livable pace.
4. Target audience: Busy wives and mothers.
5. Market ideas: Denominational magazines, women's magazines, family magazines.
6. Form: Narrative with five summary points and theme conclusion.
7. Point of view: First-person intimate (I—You).
8. Tense: Past for narrative. Present for application.
9. Mood: Serious, inspirational, motivational.
10. Length: About one thousand words.

OUTLINE WORKSHEET

1. Subject: Time and energy management.
2. Working title: Slow Down and Live.
3. Theme statement: "Be still and know that I am God. . . . They that wait upon the Lord shall exchange their strength for His."
4. Outline type: Chronological-in-a-frame.
5. Lead (Opening): Standing in front of a mirror; praying for an ulcer.
6. Bridge (Transition phrase): "The trouble had begun a year earlier."
7. Development of Body:
    1. Beautiful dreams
    2. Dreams turned into nightmares—work load increased
    3. Crisis point—panicky prayer
    4. Resolution—God's answer and healing
    5. Five lessons to be shared with other overworked readers.
8. Conclusion (Summary frame):
    Present attitude toward work and rest
    Theme statement (Scripture quotations)
9. Surprise element: How God answered my panicky prayer.

ASSIGNMENT:
1. Analyze "Slow Down and Live" on page 246, using the Structural Analysis Worksheet.
2. Create an outline based on the materials you collected for your personal experience. Use the Slant Worksheet and Outline Worksheet.

162

STRUCTURAL ANALYSIS WORKSHEET————

UNITY

1. What is the theme?
2. What is the point of view?
3. What is the tense?
4. What is the mood?

COHERENCE

1. Circle all transitions.
2. Indicate logical development. Mark events in numbered sequence (1, 2, 3, . . .).

EMPHASIS

1. Mark each technical tool used with an E, followed by the number on the list of ten emphasis tools on pages 150—151; (e.g., E9 for Plot, because Plot is number 9 on the list).
2. Mark all false tools (wordiness, improper mechanical techniques, preachiness) with an X. See pages 149—150.

SLANT WORKSHEET _____

_____

Working Title

1. Subject:
2. Theme:
3. Purpose:
4. Target audience:
5. Market ideas:
6. Form:
7. Point of view:
8. Tense:
9. Mood:
10. Length:

OUTLINE WORKSHEET _____

_____

Working Title

1. Subject:
2. Working title:
3. Theme statement:
4. Outline type:
5. Lead:
6. Bridge:
7. Development: (Body)
8. Conclusion:
9. Surprise element:

Lesson Nine
Part One
What Are My Responsibilities?

Our work as writers lays upon us certain responsibilities unique to us as Christians. Those responsibilities are based on our relationships to God, ourselves, our families and friends, our readers, fellow-writers and editors.

WHAT WE OWE GOD

1. *We ought to keep his honor foremost.* If his pleasure is our goal, his honor will be our prize. We will gladly accept whatever limitations he puts on our advancement and personal recognition, as long as he can be glorified.

2. *We ought to consider ourselves his co-workers* (See 1 Corinthians 3:6 – 10). We are members of his team. He is our Leader, Motivator, Energy-source, and Master-mind.

3. *We must maintain our own spiritual growth* (See Colossians 2:6, 7). If we ignore this dimension, then we not only forfeit our right to write for others, we also find that we have nothing of value to say.

4. *We should produce quality work that is worthy of his name.* Our message can never be separated from the quality of the vehicle used to convey it to a watching world.

5. *We should develop the gifts he has given to us.* Whether ours is the gift to write letters to lonely persons or poems for friends and acquaintances or articles, books, and drama scripts for the masses, it comes from God. Accept it. Do not deny it or bury it or be overly modest about it.

WHAT WE OWE OURSELVES

1. *We ought to be honest toward both ourselves and our work.* Limit your writing to areas that you can handle with a free conscience. Refrain from expressing opinions and presenting challenges that you are not willing to live up to. Never tell stories of questionable value for the sake of selling a book or making a name for yourself. Write only those things that you believe in and feel comfortable with.

2. *We ought to maintain an attitude of confidence.* Untrained writers often slink into anonymity corners at writers' conferences. But having proceeded this far in your studies, you are well aware that God's gift qualifies you to perform with confidence, even as you continue to experiment and learn.

3. *We ought to pursue all that will lead to consistent personal development of our lives.* We need to be consistently revising our goals and pushing them out farther and farther beyond our easy grasp.

4. *We should lead a balanced life.* We need to work on all sides of life—devotional, daily living, church ministry, social, and writing—and ask God for his perfect overall perspective.

WHAT WE OWE OUR FAMILIES

This is the most important area in all our human relationships. It is also the most inescapable area and the one most likely to cause us trouble. The basic guiding principle that should direct us is the need for a priority system that insists on putting God first, family second, and ministry third.

1. *We cannot afford to let our writing compete with our families for our time.* This does not imply throwing our schedule to our children and letting them rule our lives. Rather, it means writing when the children are in bed or the husband is at work. As children grow older, we can set office hours and teach our children the value of respecting our needs and ministry in this area. Even then, it is necessary to assure them that the door is always open when they have a genuine need.

2. *We must never allow our reputations as writers to compete with family members' identities.* One of the most rewarding compliments I ever received came from one of my students: "I notice that when you are with your husband, you are no longer Ethel Herr the writer or teacher. You are simply Walter's wife." My role as Walter's wife is that of his number-one supporter, and it must always come first among the human relationships I experience.

3. *We must never make our families compete with our deadlines and typewriters for our energies.* We must resist the temptation to spend ourselves so completely at our writing that we are exhausted by the time the family comes home and needs us.

4. *We must guard family and individual privacy at all costs.* Never publish a story—regardless of how choice—that will offend the sensitivities or invade the privacy of a family member. No story is worth the sacrifice of the good will of a loved one. Our families will always be more important than the manuscripts we produce.

5. *We can pray for our families to be understanding, but never expect them to understand.* Only another writer truly understands the needs and dreams and quirks of a writer. Do not lay such a heavy expectation on your family.

168

In short, we need to remember that families exist to serve
and help one another grow. Consequently we must never
do anything to make them resent our writing ministries as
intruders into the top-priority chamber of family living.

WHAT WE OWE OUR FRIENDS

Because our friends may not be writers and may also be
envious (probably subconsciously) of our new role in the
public eye, they can be unreasonable and demanding and at
times even hostile or rude. We dare not dismiss them and turn
into recluses. We need them and they need us. But if we are
going to write, we will have to draw a new set of boundaries
around our social relationships.

1. *We must reevaluate our social contacts and ask God to give
   us wisdom in setting right priorities.* Homemakers accus-
   tomed to spending large amounts of time chatting on the
   telephone, serving on dozens of church committees, and
   going on leisurely shopping sprees have to take the ax to
   many of these old pleasurable habits. Others may have to
   drop church and community responsibilities or simply
   limit TV-viewing time.

2. *We must be frank and honest with them, while not neglecting
   them.* Let them know that your writing is not a hobby; it is
   serious business. This involves educating them, particularly
   while we are still struggling for that first paycheck. We can
   tell them that many big-name writers never even sold a
   word of their writing to an editor until they had been hard
   at work for eight years or more. If we handle this delicate
   balancing act with care, our true friends will respond well.

3. *We need to pray for our friends to be understanding.* Search
   for creative ways to give them the attention they need. Tell
   them your office hours; then do not take the phone off the
   hook. Be open to true emergency calls.

4. *We should not ask them for an evaluation of our work or
   monopolize all conversations* with talk about our writing or
   latest research project.

AN INTRODUCTION TO CHRISTIAN WRITING

5. *We must jealously guard their privacy in the same way we protect that of our own families.* Friends soon learn to look elsewhere for a warm *confidant,* if everything they tell us ends up splashed (disguised or not) across the printed page.

WHAT WE OWE OUR READERS

1. *We ought to provide them with an open sharing of ourselves under the control of the Holy Spirit.* Use your experiences as shared examples of God's goodness, not points of coercion. Do not say, "Look at what God did for me. Now go and let him do identically the same for you." Rather, say, "See what God did for me. If he can do this, he can also do for you whatever you need."

2. *We ought to be trustworthy.* Check every fact and idea for accuracy. If our readers catch us in an error, they will be reticent to trust us through another story. Be true to life, to yourself, and to your convictions. Avoid sensationalism for the sake of a sale.

3. *We ought to provide them something of depth and significance.* Do not write to satisfy curiosity, but to meet needs. Stimulate your reader's mind to think, his heart to love, and his whole being to act on biblical principles.

4. *We must avoid the temptation to write down to them.* If we respect their intelligence and refuse to belittle them, we can make them feel good, even when we are stimulating their consciences. Never insult a reader.

5. *We need to pray for them.* Remembering to pray for ourselves as we write may come easily. Remembering to pray for the reader after the manuscript has been paid for and published is much more difficult, but equally as important.

6. *We should take time to respond to them.* Joe Bayly once said that none of us has the right to write for the public if

we are not willing to take time to write a letter or talk on the phone with the needy persons who respond to what we have written.

7. *We should offer them beauty and hope in the spirit of gentleness.* Much modern literature majors on realism to the exclusion of either beauty or hope. Christian writers, however, must consider themselves prophets with broken hearts. As we ask God to condition our minds to think positively about human need, we will be equipped to minister to the crushed spirits who open the pages of our books and magazines in search of cures.

WHAT WE OWE OUR FELLOW-WRITERS

Writing is a lonely craft. No one can write your stories for you or hold your hand while you write them. However, you need the encouragement of kindred spirits engaged in this creative process. We all need someone who understands our long apprenticeship struggles, the urgency of recording those middle-of-the-night inspirations, and our need to write by a schedule even when we are not selling by one. Our literary co-workers are God's special gift to us, and we must treat them as such. This involves five things:

1. *We must pray for one another.* Ask them to share their burdens and requests with you, and then faithfully uphold them. We should pray for our colleagues the same things we pray for ourselves as we sit down to write.

2. *We should be ready and eager to share what we have learned.* Have you found a helpful book? A writing technique that makes the job easier or more polished? A new market your friend might like to investigate? A conference or class or seminar? Some neat source or fact that will help him with his research? Be careful not to push your ideas or discoveries on other writers. Respect their creativity and discernment by giving them the freedom to take or leave anything you offer without offending you.

3. *We should offer each other a loving, honest critique, but only when it is requested.* Learn the balance between smothering a colleague with undeserved praise and cutting him to shreds in the interest of being thorough.

4. *We need to cry together and rejoice together.* Ask God to give you a heart that sincerely cares as much for your co-worker's success as your own. Never think of him as competition, but rather as a part of the team.

5. *We need to be cautious about collaborating or writing someone else's story.* Co-authoring is a legitimate venture. For beginners, however, it is also a dangerous one. It has destroyed more than one beautiful friendship. Wait until you know the writing business well before even considering such a project.

WHAT WE OWE OUR EDITORS

Many writers feel that editors should exist only to serve just as the writer dictates. To them, editors seem to have all the advantages, and thus they all need to be lectured about writers' rights. I have talked with enough editors to know that they have reasons to feel the same way about some writers. Editors are the first to admit that they are human, have problems with their old natures, and may even occasionally treat a writer unfairly. Regardless of how great their misdeeds (and editors never bear half the likeness to Godzilla as we imagine upon reading their form rejection letters), we are not responsible for editorial character. God holds us responsible to treat every editor in a Christlike manner. This means we will do several things:

1. *We will pray for our editors.* That means we will not criticize them, jump to conclusions about them, pass on ugly rumors we hear about them, belittle them, or besmirch their reputations in any way. Make a prayer list to encourage you to pray for a different editorial staff each day of the week. Do not wait for them to do something irritating or immoral before you put them on your list. Pray preventive-

ly. Pray for maturity and wisdom, and ask God to make them giants for himself.

2. *We will offer them courtesy.* Imagine you are an editor with far more manuscripts than you can read, having to conform to the demands of your supervisors and to answer calls, complaints and unreasonable requests from all sorts of rude people. Once settled "comfortably" into vicarious shoes, you will find it amazingly easy to pour on the kindness and treat your editors like the truly special servants of God that they are.

3. *We owe them legible manuscripts.* Editors are professional craftsmen, and expect us to be the same. If our manuscripts are messy, full of errors, typed on smeary corrasable paper with an ancient typewriter ribbon or in a print so fine they need a magnifying lens to read it, the editors have legitimate reason to suspect that we are not the kind of people they can work with in a professional ministry.

4. *We will offer them large doses of patience and fairness.* This comes hard at times, especially when our prize manuscript has sat on the same editor's desk for six months and we have heard absolutely nothing. Something my mother taught me as a child helped me immensely to deal with this. "No matter what people do to you," she told me, *"never* do anything to give them just reason to point an accusing finger at you!" When I began to deal with editors, I decided that no matter what happened, I would never do or say anything to an editor that would cause him to look at my manuscript or letterhead and groan, "Oh, no, not her again!" I have failed a few times, but at least this remains one of my strong guiding principles.

5. *We will send them an occasional word of encouragement.* Some business-oriented writers I know of recommend that we never waste time writing thank-you notes or anything else that does not contribute directly to a new sale. As Christians, we are expected to live by a different standard. Our Bible tells us to encourage one another, build one an-

other up (Romans 14:19; 1 Thessalonians 5:14, 15). God intended us to include editors in putting these words into practice. I have done it on many occasions, only to find that my few words brightened some editor's day, gave him a new lease on his ministry, and strengthened our working/ministering bond. Such experiences renew my convictions that my efforts are not wasted time. Moreover, they validate my writing as a ministry that goes far beyond that of a writing career.

Lesson Nine
Part Two
Writing Irresistible Leads and Titles

The first paragraph of your story needs a hook so enticing and compelling that even the most casual reader cannot resist it. Lacking this, you can forget the rest. All your thorough research, unusual facts, flawless structure, and logical outline will be wasted if your lead fails to reach out, grab your reader, and pull him into the story.

Think of your lead as your "display window" designed to coax the reader indoors where he can sample the literary delights you have prepared for him. If your window is attractive, your shop will be crowded. If it is shabby, the greatest response you can expect is a yawn and a hurried step on to the next bookcover or article.

THE LEAD

The opening sentence, paragraph, or scene of any form of writing is called the *lead*.

Two examples—one boring, the other, effective:

(1) On a sunny Sunday afternoon, my husband and I had an interesting experience which taught us the true in-depth

meaning of Sunday. Through this one experience we learned how to celebrate the Lord's Day.

(2) "Once upon a Sunday my husband and I tried a glorious experiment. It was triggered by some very simple things: a newspaper story, a horn that was blown three times, and a needle."[2]

Given the choice of these two story leads, which would you follow? Why? Analyze your reactions and decide what makes one dull, the other attractive.

IMPACT OF AN EFFECTIVE LEAD ON THE READER

(See the Fiction Plot Pattern diagram on page 177 to learn how the lead is related to other parts of a properly structured story. Note that while personal experience stories are not fiction, they need to be structured like fiction.)

An effective lead:
1. Gets the reader's attention.
2. Makes him care about what you have to say.
3. Tells him what your subject is—introduces the problem or conflict or controversy that lies at the heart of your plot structure.
4. Either provides a frame for your story or simply launches the reader directly into the story.
5. Hooks him. He reads it and says, "I have to know the rest."

KINDS OF LEADS

While there are almost limitless types, most fall into five basic categories:
1. *Narrative*—tells a story.
2. *Descriptive*—paints a sensory or mood picture as a story setting.
3. *Thematic*—introduces a thesis.
4. *Quotation*—quotes some well-known person.
5. *Question*—draws the reader into the story by asking him a question.

Each type has many subtypes. Here are examples of a few:

FICTION PLOT PATTERN

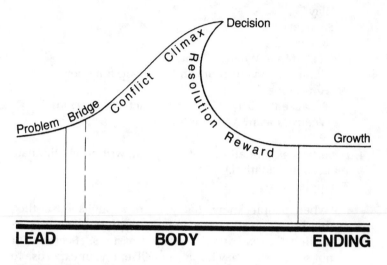

NARRATIVE LEADS

1. *Narration* (Beginning of your story).
   Example:

   > A lone widow stooped over the field outside of Zare-phath. She pulled at a clump of sun-baked grasses until their pithy stems yielded to the grasp of her twiglike fingers. She tucked the drought-sparse fuel under her left arm, and prepared to reach for another bunch. A husky voice startled her from behind: "Peace be with you, woman. . . . Ho there!"[3]

2. *Anecdotal.*
   Example:

   > I once heard of a man who prayed in a most unusual way. Every morning he picked up a pencil and a pad of paper and wrote a long "letter to God." Then, folding the document, he took it to his fireplace and set it afire. As smoke rose from the curling piece of paper, he envisioned his prayer ascending heavenward.

3. *Dialogue*.
    Example:

> "Ray!"
> Silence.
> "Raymond!"
> "Yeah, Mom. Whadya want?"
> "Come clean your room so I can mop the floor."
> "How come?"
> "Because it's dirty. Why else? In fact, it's atrocious."
> "Whadya mean? My room's clean."

4. *Hypothetical*. (Situation that is typical; written to stimulate reader's imagination.)
    Example:

> "When people know that you are a published author, they bring you all sorts of interesting and sometimes perplexing "undiscovered literary treasures." Secretly (or not so secretly) they hope you will lend your expertise to help them get these obvious gems out into full view of a waiting world."[4]

DESCRIPTIVE LEADS

1. *Setting*.
    Example:

> "A thousand royal palms lined the highway to King Solomon's hilltop palace. Their shaggy fronds barely stirred in the still-hot midnight air and cast lethargic shadow-patterns against the polished gold and marble portico. The silence of the sleeping estate was broken only by the muffled slapping of four pacing sandaled feet and the periodic mumble of two baritone voices."[5]

2. *Characterization*.
    Example:

> "Grandma had a streak of mischief. I'll never forget the day she put it to work teaching me, as a young bride, a valuable lesson."[6]

3. *Mood.*
   Example:

> "A golden pre-dawn haze hung over Jerusalem at day-break. Shallum stepped out of his mud-brick house and inhaled the morning-fragrant air. Already the city was astir with shouting and laughter, the rattling of pots, and the clopping of animal hooves. The middle-aged city official strode into the street, turned a full circle, and surveyed the completed new stone-and-brick horizon of the city silhouetted against a lightening sky."[7]

THEMATIC LEADS

1. *Thesis.*
   Example:

> "Memorial Day is for remembering. How you celebrate it depends on what you remember."[8]

2. *Startling Statement.*
   Example:

> "I never attend church."[9] (Note, this is startling because it appears in a denominational church magazine. The audience determines the startling value.)

3. *Factual.*
   Example:

> Education costs money—lots of money! To educate one pupil for a school year in 1978–79 cost between $1,200 in Arkansas and $3,900 in Alaska. During the past ten years, public education costs have "increased 187 percent, more than twice the rate of other consumer goods and services."[10]

4. *Problem.*
   Example:

> "Vacation Bible School in our church had lost its zing."[11]

180

QUOTATION LEADS

1. *Famous Person.*
   Example:

   > "Mark Twain once said that 'education is what you must acquire without any interference from your schooling.'"[12]

2. *Literary Quote.*
   Example:

   > "Once upon a time there were three Bears. . . . One of them was a Little, Wee, Small bear and one was a Middle-sized Bear, and one was a Great, Huge Bear. . . ."[13]

3. *Testimonial.*
   Example:

   > "'He's real for sure,' Reesa keeps repeating as she gives her testimony."[14]

QUESTION LEAD

Example:

> "Did you ever reach desperation circle?"[15]

WRITING AN EFFECTIVE LEAD

Leads are the most difficult part of any piece you will ever write. Some writers claim that if you give them a well-written, snappy lead they can guarantee to give you a good article. You may spend more time rewriting the lead than any other part of your story. Here is how to go about it:

1. *Make a study of leads in all you read.* Decide whether they are good or bad and what makes them that way. If bad, ask how they could be improved. Practice rewriting them. Make a collection of good leads. Label them according to types.

2. *Think of your audience and plan an attention-getting lead.* Take into consideration your reader's interests, education

level, attention span, and needs. For example, do not start a children's story with a dry rehearsal of facts or some theological definition. Preferably start with action or dialogue.

3. *Pick a lead that fits the theme of your piece.*
   a. Begin *action stories* with action scenes.
   b. Begin *mood stories* with mood settings.
   c. Begin *character sketches* with characterization.
   d. Begin *inspirational articles* with an anecdote that introduces a problem to be solved.

4. *Pick a lead that fits the mood of your piece.* For example, do not start a serious treatise on handling grief with a humorous anecdote.

5. *Pick a lead that fits the pace of your piece.* For example, do not begin a slow-moving mood piece with a snappy anecdote.

6. *Pick a lead that fits the style of the piece.* For example, do not start out chatty and then turn formal or intellectual.

The important common guideline in numbers 2−6 above is this: *Never promise one thing and deliver another.*

7. *Make the lead interesting and irresistible.* Remember that the function of your lead is to attract a reader who may have no good reason to care about what you have written. If you approach him dully, he will move on.

8. *Make the lead significant.* Promise the reader something he cares about.

9. *Begin at an interesting place in the action of a story.* Begin where something exciting or provocative is happening— the point where things are beginning to change and the problem is becoming evident or perhaps at the height of a crisis.

10. *Fit your lead into the overall chronological pattern of your story.*

a. *Straight chronology:* Begins at the beginning and goes on in sequence as the story happened.

b. *Flashback* or *frame chronology:* Begins at some problem or crisis point, then flashes back to the sequential beginning and continues chronologically.

11. *Experiment with different types of leads to find the most suitable one.*

EXAMPLES OF DIFFERENT LEAD TYPES FOR "ASSIGNMENT AT SUNSET" (on pages 244–246):

1. *Narrative Leads.*
   a. *Narration:*
      Example:

   > Cool bay breezes were just beginning to stir around us on that hot July evening. From my chaise lounge on the patio, I heard the telephone ring. Reluctant to be disturbed, I groaned, then made my way into an overly warm house.

   b. *Dialogue:*
      Example:

   > "Ethel," a familiar voice came through my telephone receiver, "I had to call you. It's been a dreadful day. I feel like I've been walking a tightrope and finally fell off."
   >
   > Panic seized me as my disturbed friend now fell silent. "Was it really worse than yesterday?" I countered lamely.

2. *Descriptive Leads.*
   a. *Setting:*
      Example:

   > One warm July evening, we were sitting on the patio, basking in the cool bay breezes just beginning to stir through the trees around us. Summer had finally

arrived. While we'd anticipated its warmth far longer than usual, it hit us so suddenly that we had wilted.

b. *Characterization:*
Example:

When my friend Betty called me, I noted that her voice was tight and distraught. Just like the night before, she talked about her three teenaged boys with their problems . . . about her parents who always intruded into her personal affairs . . . about her third husband and their recent divorce . . . about her physical and mental weaknesses and that horrible feeling of never being able to cope with it all. She reminded me of a child with a wounded spirit—always wanting consolation, but fearful to reach out and ask for it, hesitant to receive it.

c. *Mood:*
Example:

On a hot July evening the air was bustling with exciting new vacation plans. Summer had finally arrived that week—very late indeed. And the heat felt good, but overwhelmed us a bit. I reclined in my chaise lounge on the patio, sipping iced lemonade, watching the antics of our newest kitten, and exchanging trivialities with my husband and the children. The last thing I wanted that evening was to be routed from my comfortable retreat.

3. *Thematic Leads.*
a. *Startling Statement.*
Example:

When God called me to do a job for Him one hot July evening, I immediately refused.

b. *Thesis.*
Example:

It always pays to move out when God gives you a job to do—even if you haven't the foggiest notion how to do it.

c. *Factual.*
  Example:

> Sometimes God asks me to do things I do not know how to do—such as comforting a woman who has just gone through her second divorce and does not how how to manage her three rambunctious teen-age boys. I have never been divorced, I do not have three boys, and I get very tongue-tied when anyone asks me for advice about something I have never experienced. Besides, I have never had any counseling training.

4. *Quotation Lead.*
  Example:

> "When he putteth forth his own sheep he goeth before them." This Bible quotation never had real meaning for me until a hot July evening.

5. *Question Lead.*
  Example:

> What would you do if the mother of your son's best friend called to tell you that she was falling apart and had no more ideas for coping with life?

My choice for this article was *Narration.*

Dialogue sidestepped my delightful pre-telephone-call situation and made it look as if my friend's problem were the story problem.

Description focused on nonessentials of the setting and was too slow starting.

Characterization again focused on my friend's problem, not mine.

Mood was too slow getting into the problem. It might have been all right if I had been doing a longer piece, but this article was short and had to be to the point.

Startling Statement, Thesis, and *Factual* gave the piece a teaching flavor. Besides, *Startling Statement* was not an accurate account of my reaction; it was padded for shock value.

Quotation was also teachy and a bit ordinary.

Question brought the reader into dialogue with me, and I did not want that. My purpose was to share an experience, carrying the reader through it with me, so that he or she could experience it in the way and in the sequence that I did and come out saying, "How great God is to solve the problems which come our way!"

TITLES

While the title will be the first thing your reader sees, it may be the last thing you settle on. And once you do create one that suits you, the editor may change it completely. Titles work either for or against you, even in advance of your lead. They sell your story to the reader as he scans the table of contents or flips through the pages of a magazine searching for those things that will reward him for the time he spends in their company.

ELEMENTS OF A GOOD TITLE

1. *It is brief* (preferably five words or less). Short poignant, pithy titles grab unwary readers and captivate them for your story.

2. *It is appropriate.* Relating to the mood and the theme of the article or story, it gives some honest clue to the content of the piece. It is unforgivable to promise "Ten Easy Steps to Better Health" and then tell us only how you found better health.

3. *It is specific.* General titles such as "The Reformation" do little to arouse interest. Nor do they give an accurate idea of content. When we apply the Zoom Lens Technique and the title becomes "Women Who Sparked the Reformation" or something provocative such as "Was the Reformation a Spiritual Movement?" the magnetic effect increases 100 per cent.

4. *It arrests attention.* It must jump off the page into the reader's heart and mind. Good titles never blend into the

page, saying little, promising nothing, looking limp and life-less.

5. *It relies on active verbs and concrete nouns.* Adverbs, weak adjectives, and unnecessary connectives are deadly in titles. Every word counts in this strategic bit of show-and-tell writing.

6. *It is fresh, original, and alive.* Nothing turns off a prospective reader like a trite title such as "Storming Those Pearly Gates in Search of Lost Souls."

ASSIGNMENT:

1. Read five articles in a recent issue of the *Reader's Digest.* Answer the following questions about their leads and titles:
   a. What types are they?
   b. Do they grab your attention?
   c. Do they make you care?
   d. Do they give you an honest promise of what the article holds?
2. Using all the notes you have written about your personal experience and the outline you have planned, experiment with different lead types, keeping in mind the focus and theme you want to emphasize. Settle on one lead. Write it as well as you can, revising it until it pleases you or until you do not know what else to do with it.
3. Experiment with a title, choosing one or more tentative ones.

---

[1] Romans 14:19; 1 Thessalonians 5:14, 15.

[2] Mary Margaret Kern, "An Old Fashioned Sunday," *The Lutheran,* May 1975.

[3] Ethel Herr, *Chosen Families,* p. 75.

[4] Ethel Herr, *How Long Has It Been Since You Prayed for an Editor?* Scheduled for publication by Still Point Press.

[5] Ethel Herr, *Chosen Families,* p. 65.

[6] Ethel Herr, "Give and Let Give," *Family Life Today,* December 1975, p. 10.

[7] Ethel Herr, *Chosen Families,* p. 91.

[8]Ethel Herr, "What Do You Remember on Memorial Day?" *Applied Christianity,* May 1974, p. 27.

[9]Ethel Herr, "No Place for Outsiders," *The Evangelical Beacon,* February 13, 1968, p. 10. (Printed as *Anonymous)*

[10]Ethel Herr, *Schools: How Parents Can Make a Difference,* p. 101.

[11]Ethel Herr, "New Approach for VBS," *The Standard,* March 15, 1977, p. 27.

[12]Ethel Herr, *Schools: How Parents Can Make a Difference,* p. 31.

[13]Ibid., p. 121.

[14]Fred Prinzing, "He's Real for Sure," *The Standard,* September 21, 1970, p. 11.

[15]Ethel Herr, "Rags and a Prayer," *Today,* March 18, 1973, p. 4.

Lesson Ten
Part One
How Do I Develop a Writing Style?

This is one of the first questions many beginning writers ask. They have the mistaken idea that however well they learn to write, the future holds nothing but a maze of blind alleys for them unless they can find a "style." When asked what they mean by style, they usually give a vague answer about some unidentifiable mystical qualities that earmark literature with class and prestige.

To all such students, the truth should bring great freedom of mind. Style is not mystical. Nor does it have to be coaxed into existence by long and arduous effort at imitating the masters. In fact, quite like happiness, as long as you pursue it, it will probably elude you. Once you set your mind to learning the disciplines of good technique and practicing all the rules you have learned so far in this course, style will emerge. You cannot stop it.

STYLE DEFINED

Precisely what, then, is style? It has been defined in many ways, by many kinds of writers.

Robert Frost calls it "the way a man takes himself."[1] Others describe it in the following ways:

190

" . . . the distinctive manner in which an author uses language; his choice of words and their arrangement to express a special tone, attitude, or manner."[2]

" . . . a nice surprise. It comes more as a gift than acquisition. . . . Style always has a secret that we want."[3]

" . . . the imprint of the author's personality on subject matter. . . ."[4]

Basically effective style is the interaction of the writer's unique personality and talents with significant ideas expressed memorably on paper with the assistance of disciplined technique. True, not all styles reflect discipline. A slovenly, inartistic attempt to communicate may be classified as a style of sorts. But it is not effective, and marks its author as an untrained amateur.

ASPECTS OF GOOD STYLE

What characterizes good style?

1. *Style is personal.* "It is never in two human beings the same," writes Sidney Cox.[5] Like a fingerprint, it is yours and yours alone. Since it is so personal, the writer must take care to insure that it expresses his person in a natural, unaffected manner.

   Avoid stiltedness, inappropriate formality, attempts to impress readers with your great learning or piety. Make it an honest representation of your genuine self. Be yourself and tell the truth on paper. Resist the temptation to write what the reader wants to hear regardless of what you believe about your subject.

   Further, being personal implies *originality.* Do not try to imitate the style of your favorite author. On the other hand, do not strive so hard for originality that you become phony or ludicrous. There are many types of style—philosophical, cynical, flowery, dignified, conversational, anecdotal, picturesque, formal, humorous, textbookish, carefree, arduous, breezy, preachy—just for starters. Depending on what you write and who your audience is, you may employ many or all of these different styles at different times in your writing. Regardless of which type you use, if you are being natural, honest, and original, everything you write will bear the inimitable stamp of your own personality—it will be *your own style*.

Finally, because style is personal, it is a *growing* thing. It expresses you. Hence, it grows and matures as you grow and mature both personally and technically. I like the way Faith Baldwin explains this phenomenon. "Style," she says, "is like a signature." A child's first signature is far from perfect, and usually not terribly distinctive. As he grows and practices, he develops his own "stylish" signature, not identical to any other in the world. Strive to make your style serve as the identifying autograph with which you mark everything you write as an expression of your growing person.

2. *Style communicates.* It functions as a bridge that meets the reader on one side of an idea and carries him smoothly and safely to the other side. In order to do this, your writing must be *clear.* Only a rare reader will bother to stay with what you have written if your meaning is so obscure that he has to labor long over it.

Good style must be *simple.* Hence, avoid wordiness, complex arrangements of words, sentences, paragraphs, and ideas. Effective style also has *force.* It puts the emphasis in the right places and stimulates the reader to think, to feel, to act. Communicating style also has *color.* It avoids trite terminology; dull, fuzzy, antiquated photographs; boring treatises; and pedagogical sermons.

3. *Style fits.* Whether you are breezy, didactic, humorous, or ponderous depends on your subject, your purpose, and your audience. Learn to be flexible, and allow your personality to fuse with many different moods on paper.

Effective style has a number of literary components. One is *technical accuracy.* Grammar, usage, punctuation, and paragraphing, sound structure (unity, coherence, and emphasis), literary excellence (proper use of the tools of literature)—all need to be polished to your highest possible degree of correctness.

I have read manuscripts that scored nearly 100 percent

192

on this component, but were still unpublishable. There are other things needed for good style as well—things such as *variety and balance.* Vary your sentences. Do not use all simple declarative sentences. Write interrogatory (questions), exclamatory, and complex sentences. Vary their length—some short, some long. Structure them differently. Do not begin or end them all the same way.

Vary the literary forms you use. In this course, we have concentrated on learning to write narrative, which tells a story. However, in order to develop a winning style, you also need to work on three other basic forms: (1) *description,* which paints sensory pictures, (2) *exposition,* which explains, informs, interprets, defines, and gives directions, and (3) *argumentation,* which attempts to persuade the reader to action or belief and to motivate him to action. (See Appendix for further helps and exercises in learning these and other literary forms.)

Another component of effective style is the *personal element* produced by dialogue, direct quotes, anecdotes, and occasional touches of humor. These are the things that reach out and grab your readers. People always respond more readily to people than to impersonal ideas or to abstract truths. Experiment with ways to increase the human factor in your writing style.

Effective style also employs *suspense.* It does not blow the punch line in the first paragraph. Nor does it wait until the final paragraph to introduce a problem and solve it. Instead, by the use of the proper arrangement of facts, effective style builds toward a climax and sustains interest. It makes the reader care and satisfies him that your logic is sound. If your style fails this criterion, your reader will not follow you, regardless of how sturdy the other components of your communication bridge across the idea chasm.

Finally, good style uses *lively and varied vocabulary.* Wear out your dictionary and thesaurus. Read with one eye wide open for words. Listen to every conversation with the same beachcombing mentality.

Are you discouraged at this point? Take heart. Apart from adherence to certain writing rules, which you are already working on, there is little rightness or wrongness to style. It is, remember, something that grows with your person and with practice. This brings us back to our original question: How can you develop a writing style?

SIX BASIC STEPS TO IMPROVING STYLE

While it is true that style happens when we polish our skills and practice our craft, six basic steps can help us both to change the amateurish sloppy patterns that come naturally to all beginning writers and to begin nourishing the growth of positive, effective styles.

1. *Read.* Read as much as you can and still take time to live, relate, research, and write. Read diversely, critically, and on occasion, aloud. Style is often better heard than seen.

2. *Observe.* "The first step in improving your writing is to improve your observing."[6] Watch people at work, at play, in meditative moods, in relationship situations, at worship. Listen to people talking. Become a student of God's person and his ways first, then of modern man in all his complexities.

3. *Think and pray.* Let your readings and your observations and your experiences of life challenge old thinking patterns and start you on the road to growing attitudes. Ask God for divine originality and perspective. Let him change you from within and he will freshen and deepen your style.

> The more we get what we now call "ourselves" out of the way and let Him take us over, the more truly ourselves we become. There is so much of Him that millions and millions of "little Christs," all different will still be too few to express Him fully. . . .
>
> Until you have given up yourself to Him you will not have a real self. Sameness is to be found most among the most "natural" men, not among those who surrender to Christ. How monotonously alike all the great tyrants and conquerors have been; how gloriously different are the saints.[7]

194

4. *Study.* Learn the rules; study examples of clear, effective communicating style. Master the principles found in *The Elements of Style* by Strunk and White. Purchase, study, and refer often to *Write Right* by Jan Venolia. (See Recommended reading on page 235.)

5. *Aim for plainness.* Included in this are simplicity, orderliness, and sincerity.

6. Finally, *write, write, write.* . . . The result? Quietly, imperceptibly, uniquely, the real YOU will emerge on paper. You will have style.

Lesson Ten
Part Two
Writing Captivating Middles and Memorable Endings

Your irresistible lead will lure the reader from the voices of a hundred competitors—family demands, personal problems, the calculatedly attractive media, and lethargy. You accomplish this difficult feat by making some personal and appealing promises.

Well done, or rather, well begun! For you have assumed an obligation to carry through on what you promised. Now you must make your story every bit as significant and pleasant as you led him to believe it would be, to make him glad that he chose your story to read. You will do this by continuing with a captivating middle and wrapping it up in a memorable ending.

THE CAPTIVATING MIDDLE

The middle is the body of your story—the logical succession of events that builds toward a climax. It is the demonstration of your merchandise as you advertised it in your "display window" lead.

CHARACTERISTICS OF A GOOD MIDDLE

1. *Smooth flow.* Never make it necessary for the reader to re-read anything in order to keep his bearings. A good way to check this is to give your manuscript to a friend to read aloud. Watch and listen to him carefully as he reads. If he stops, stumbles, looks puzzled, or rereads at any point, make a note of it. This spot needs smoothing out.

2. *Ability to sustain interest.* Keep it fascinating.
   a. Omit unnecessary words, irrelevant ideas, off-the-track stories, lengthy descriptions, long dialogue, or rambling thoughts. Stay on the rails NO MATTER WHAT.
   b. Keep things moving. Intersperse physical action with thoughts, descriptions, and dialogue. Describe people and places in terms of action rather than relying solely on adjectives and flowery pictures.

3. *Logical development.* Build gradually but continuously toward the climax of your story.

4. *Consistent style.* While you may insert light touches of humor even in more serious stories, do it gently, not giving the impression that you are trying to be cute. Do not change style mid-story.

5. *Faithfulness to the central theme.* Never allow your reader to miss the one point you are trying to make. You may build gradually to the point, and your reader may not know what it is until he reaches the climax. But resist the temptation to meander among tantalizing related points when you need to zero in on reaching your main theme goal.

COMPONENTS OF A GOOD MIDDLE

1. *Three main structural parts.* (Refer to Fiction Plot Pattern diagram on page 177.)
   a. *Bridge:* the section that carries the reader from the *lead* into the *body* in such a way that he makes the connection naturally.

b. *Conflict:* a series of conflicts between either:
   Man and God
   Man and nature
   Man and man
   Man and self.
   These conflicts build in intensity toward a climax.

c. *Climax:* the point where conflict reaches its peak and characters are ready for a resolution. It usually ends with the main character making a critical decision that opens the door for the resolution.

2. *Technical tools used in middles.*
   a. *Series of scenes in a story or points in an article:* Each scene or point draws the reader more deeply into your experience or idea. Scenes should be filled with action and/or conflict, and should contribute to the progressive unfolding of the plot.

   b. *Effective transitions:* These may be single words (such as *finally, in that case, at last*) or whole sentences or paragraphs (as the bridge between *lead* and *body*). Their function is to make smooth connections between ideas, scenes, or words.

      Study transitions in all you read. Make lists of effective ones. Note what makes them either effective or weak.

   c. *Flashbacks:* These may be stories or scenes from the past, used only when essential to do one or both of two things:
      1) Give background information needed for the reader to understand present action.
      2) Provide adequate motivation so the reader sympathizes with and/or understands why the characters of your story act the way they do.

   CAUTIONS:
      1) Use flashbacks sparingly. Too many confuse the reader and spoil continuity of story.
      2) Keep them short. Long flashbacks create confusion and sidetrack the reader.
      3) Introduce them with proper transitions so that the reader has no question how they relate to the chronology of the main story.

d. *Dialogue:* Conversation between characters is an effective means to:
  1) Reveal character
  2) Further action
  3) Increase "show" value of the story.

e. *Description:* Use sparingly. Keep it short, lively, active, and colorful. Break it up and enhance it with appropriate bits of interspersed dialogue and action.

f. *Explanation:* Short commentaries, definitions, and facts pertinent for understanding.

RULES FOR WRITING GOOD MIDDLES

1. *Make them smooth.* Remember your goal is to carry the reader along irresistibly so he cannot bring himself to lay your story down.

2. *Plan the scene sequence carefully.* One scene (or point in an article) should grow logically out of another so that the reader is adequately prepared for the climax and resolution. Use transitions carefully. Sometimes you need not talk about all that transpires between scenes; simply end one scene and begin the next. Most often, however, you will need a transition word or sentence to connect the two.

3. *Fulfill what your lead promises.* If, for example, you promise to tell your reader how to overcome fear, don't then tell about your own battle with it and conclude by praising God for delivering you. Your story and your praise are valid, but you promised to tell your reader how to handle his own problem. In that case, you must give him specific suggestions and illustrate them with ways that your technique has worked for you. Then you can conclude with a reminder that no matter how hard he works at it, every person needs to give God credit for making the methods work.

4. *Gather sufficient material.* Make sure you have all the material you need to write a substantial story. If your story falls flat, you may need more facts or color. Perhaps your story is

not strong enough to bear its own weight as a full story, but would do well as an illustrative anecdote.

5. *Write in specifics, not generalities.* SHOW—do not merely tell. In my introductory chapter for *Growing Up Is a Family Affair,* I told the story of a difficult day when I lost my temper with my children. When I began to write the chapter, I tried to portray my anger with some hedging generalities such as "I felt my anger getting bigger and bigger, until it frightened me."

My critique group refused to let me gloss over that painful-to-relive scene. "We want to see and feel your anger," they insisted. They prodded me on through many rewrites until I had turned generalities into specifics by sharing explosive emotions, rough actions, escalating voice, barked commands, white-fisted knuckles, and trembling reactions —in short, a wealth of details.

6. *Avoid irrelevant trivia.* Trivia sidetracks the reader and diverts the flow of your story.

7. *Keep technical tools in proper balance.* Action, dialogue, description, scenes, flashbacks, transitions, and explanations need to work together. Blend them into a unified, well-orchestrated composition.

THE MEMORABLE ENDING
The ending of the story is the conclusion—the goal toward which the whole story has been moving.

PURPOSE OF THE ENDING

1. *It ties up loose threads.* It may also leave them in such a form that the reader can tie them himself. An ending puts the finishing touches on the drama and suspense built up through the story. It resolves conflicts, draws conclusions, makes projections. This is often accomplished by repeating or referring to some part of your lead in the concluding paragraph.

Examples:

> Lead: "Did you ever reach desperation circle?"
> Ending: "Often I stumble, as a reminder that my useful-
> ness was won by Jesus Christ in a battle at desperation
> circle."[8]

2. *It pleases and satisfies the reader.* Unresolved or shoddy
   endings bore the reader, disappoint him, frustrate him, or
   leave a bad taste in his mouth. A good ending leaves him
   with a provocative, reassuring, or challenging thought. Do
   not forget your mission to dispense hope.

3. *It inspires the reader to increased faith in God and positive
   action.*

COMPONENTS OF AN ENDING

(Refer to Fiction Plot Pattern diagram from Lesson 9, page 177.)

1. *Resolution.* The conflict of your story has been settled. This
   happens most effectively if it comes as a direct or indirect
   result of some decision or action on the part of your main
   character. In many Christian stories, legitimate resolutions
   come when we stop trying to figure them out and let God
   show us the answers. Often these provide delightful surprise endings.

2. *Reward or punishment.* This comes as a result of the resolution of the conflict. The reward is for right decisions and
   actions; the punishment is for wrong decisions or unwise
   disobedient action. If undeserved mercy rewards wrong
   decisions and/or actions, show some positive reaction or
   change of heart on the part of the person receiving mercy.

3. *Growth.* The main character grows because of the circumstances and actions of the story. What has he learned? How
   is he a better person? How is he better prepared to handle
   life the next time he faces difficulties? How has his recep-
   tion of undeserved mercy made him a more devoted Chris-

tion or merciful person? How has his trial increased his
faith or made him a more effective servant of Jesus Christ?

KINDS OF ENDINGS

1. *Summary ending.*
   Example:

> "Today I look back and remember it all as the Christmas
> when God showed me His love in a special way—love
> that reaches down into life's dark moments and sur-
> prises us with rare treats of beauty."[9]

2. *Challenge ending.*
   Example:

> "Someday in our separate searching for reality, we may
> become desperate enough and bold enough to try the
> church again. Perhaps your church.
>
> "But I wonder, when and if we should, would there be
> a place for us in your church, because you have made a
> place for us in your heart?"[10]

3. *Projection ending.*
   Example:

> "I slipped the tiny necklace into my purse—to stay until
> I should find my answer. And I had a warm feeling it
> wouldn't be long."[11]

4. *Punch line ending.*
   Example:

> P.S. Don't burn your letters! God can read them in your
> notebook, and you will need to do the same.

5. *Thesis ending.*
   Example:

> "'O God,' I prayed. 'You are achieving in that young lady
> of ours what all the parental example in the world could
> never accomplish alone. Thanks to You, she's excited
> about Jesus Christ! Forgive me for ever thinking I could
> do your job, O Master Teacher.'"

When writing articles, you can use at least two other techniques effectively:

6. *Quotation ending.* Particularly good if from some well-known person or authority on the subject you are writing about.

7. *Anecdote ending.* This illustrates the main theme of your article.

RULES FOR WRITING GOOD ENDINGS

1. *Stop when the story is over.* Do not rehash your message or give unnecessary details that happened after the story ended.

2. *Suit the mood and atmosphere of the ending to the overall story.*

3. *Make the ending memorable.* Write it with such appeal that the reader can never forget your theme.

4. *Tie the ending to the story theme.* Make it appear to grow naturally out of the story as a last-shot sharing of your theme.

5. *Try to use a surprise element.* Good stories usually do not have predictable endings. However, they need to:
   a. Be believable.
   b. Be prepared for. Plant the seeds of your ending, preferably in the lead, so that while the reader does not expect your ending, he can always look back and say, "Why, of course, I should have guessed!"

6. *"Be brisk, be brief, be gone."*[12]

ASSIGNMENT:

1. Read the story "Then Came Christmas" on p. 251 and study its Plan Worksheet and the Structural Pattern outline. Note

how the various story elements conform to the instructions in this lesson.

2. Take the five stories or articles you read in *Reader's Digest* for the last lesson and answer the following questions about each ending:

What type of ending is it?

Does it tie up all the loose threads?

Does it satisfy you? If not, why not?

Does it surprise you? Was the solution properly planted?

Is it memorable?

3. Write the rest of your personal experience story, keeping in mind the things we discussed about middles and endings.

[1] Cox, *Indirections*, p. 48.

[2] *This Is America*, eds., Harold H. Wagenheim, Matthew Dolkey & Donald G. Kobler (New York: Henry Holt & Co., 1956), p. 261.

[3] Cox, *Indirections*, p. 49.

[4] Harry Shaw, *A Collection of Readings for Writers*, 6th ed. (New York: Harper & Row Publishers, Inc., 1967), p. 6.

[5] Cox, *Indirections*, p. 49.

[6] Fred Morgan, *Here and Now* (New York: Harcourt, Brace and World, 1968), p. 1.

[7] From pages 189, 190 of *Mere Christianity* by C. S. Lewis. (Copyright 1943, 1945, 1952 by Macmillan Publishing Co., Inc. Copyright renewed.) Used by permission.

Material from *Mere Christianity* by C. S. Lewis is used by permission of William Collins & Co. Ltd., London. © C. S. Lewis PTE Ltd., 1952.

[8] Ethel Herr, "Rags and a Prayer," p. 8.

[9] Ethel Herr, "Then Came Christmas," *Home Life*, December 1974, p. 36.

[10] Ethel Herr, "No Place for Outsiders," p. 11.

[11] Ethel Herr, "I Took Off My Badge," *The Young Calvinist*, March 1970, p. 5.

[12] Lee Wyndham, *Writing for Children and Teen-agers* (Cincinnati: Writer's Digest, 1968), p. 125.

PLAN WORKSHEET

Then Came Christmas

Working Title

1. Theme sentence:
   God saves His special delights for life's darkest moments.
2. Lead:
   Critical situation—Wally is in pain. Fog outside. Difficult decision. (Number 5 in story sequence)
3. Bridge:
   My thoughts and reminiscences that bring me to this point.
4. Body (Middle):
   a. John and Pauline come to visit
   b. Wally pops out with chicken pox
   c. Miserable week follows
   d. Christmas Eve celebration
   e. Lead
   f. Prayer for forgiveness for complaining
   g. Critical situation repeated
5. Ending:
   Snow discovered; Wally feels better. Summary of what I learned through the experience.
6. Twist (Surprise element):
   God blessed me when I least deserved or expected it, giving me a treasured lifetime memory.
7. Special effects tools:
   Dutch pea soup
   Snow plant
   My thoughts and prayers

STRUCTURAL PATTERN

Then Came Christmas
Working Title

LEAD	Scene 1: Critical situation
	Background information—Dutch pea soup
BRIDGE	Transition: My thoughts—"What a way to spend Christmas . . ."
	Flashback to beginning of story
	Scene 2: Touring Holland with family visitors
	Problem plant: Wally's stomachache
	Transition: "Tour duty over"
	Solution plant: Snowflakes
BODY	Scene 3: Chicken pox discovery
(MIDDLE)	Background information: the kids already had them
	Transition: "the days that followed"
	Scene 4: Miserable week (told by factual narration)
	Transition: "Come Christmas Eve, *however*. . . ."
	Scene 5: Christmas Eve (told by factual narration)
	Transition: "Several hours later. . . ."
	Scene 6: Bedroom critical situation revived
	Prayer for forgiveness
	Transition: "I must have dozed. . . ."
	Critical problem repeated. Climax decision reached.
ENDING	Transition: "Nothing that night had prepared me. . . ."
	Surprise solution (Resolution) and our reactions (Reward)
	Summary of resulting action
	Growth—lesson learned

Lesson Eleven
Part One
What Do I Do with My Completed Manuscript?

Congratulations! You have just arrived at a place in your writing career investigation that many aspiring writers never reach. You have come to the end of your rough draft and have perhaps even penned across the bottom of the page in caligraphic script, the distinguished message: "FINIS." What now?

Put it in a drawer and forget about it.

Forget my brainchild? you think. *When the world needs it so desperately* NOW?

Or perhaps your reaction is more like this: *Gladly!* It turned out so terribly you think you ought to sell your typewriter and turn to something profitable.

Regardless of how you feel about your work at the end of your rough draft, it is neither ready for the editorial desk nor the wastebasket. It needs to cool off. You cannot possibly begin to see it objectively for at least another week.

The journey from inspiration to publication is a long one. Few of the steps can be rushed. Writing is an art and must grow at its own pace. Further, you are dealing with business-like editors in a competitive marketplace.

At this point, it helps to chart the route from idea to printed page and take a good look at the steps we have not yet dealt with in our studies.

IDEA TO PUBLICATION

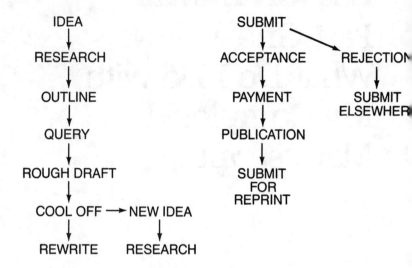

THE QUERY

Once you have written a number of articles and have an accurate feel for your capabilities, you will write a query letter to an editor before writing an article. In a query letter, you explain your article idea, showing its value to the reader and your ability to handle it convincingly, and you solicit the editor's interest.

Do not send queries for fiction, poetry, or short pieces, or when you have already written the article *and* your chosen editor does not require one.

Do send a query when (1) the editor requires it, (2) each magazine on your possibility list would demand a different treatment or slant, (3) the piece will involve a lot of research and/or expense which you would not pursue for any other reason, or (4) your idea is so specialized that only one market would be interested in it.

Query letters predispose an editor to read your manuscript with interest. They keep the door open for your manuscript in case someone else is doing something competitive. They may save you many hours of wasted research and/or writing of an unsalable piece. The editor's reply to a query should help you in slanting and organizing the article to suit the market.

TYPES OF QUERY LETTERS

1. *The idea query.* In this, you present a synopsis of the idea and perhaps include a couple of anecdotes, quotes, and/or facts of special interest.

2. *The outline query.* In this you present the idea and enclose an outline. Outline queries are particularly helpful if you are treating some subject which has a great number of angle possibilities.

COMPONENTS OF THE QUERY LETTER

1. *Your subject.* Include some idea of what you intend to do with it.

2. *Your specific thesis.*

3. *Your style.* Try to pinpoint your approach: anecdotal, personal experience, straight reporting, etc.

4. *Your credentials.* State what authority and ability you have to write this piece. Include writing credits, if you have any. Otherwise, give qualifications such as the type of experience you have had in the particular topic area or in general.

5. *Reader benefits.* This does not mean why you want to write the piece, but why the reader will want to read it.

6. *Questions for the editor.* These deal with how you should treat the piece—slant, word length, and the like.

7. *Photos.* Indicate whether you will send photos.

WHAT DO I DO WITH MY COMPLETED MANUSCRIPT?

8. *Time Frame.* You may or may not give some idea of how soon you plan to have the completed manuscript ready for submission.

9. *Working Title.* This is usually included in your letter.

THE ESSENTIALS OF QUERY WRITING

1. *Be prepared.* Do sufficient research ahead of time so you know where you are going. Preferably write a tentative lead before you query. Often including this lead in the query is a wise idea.

2. *Be brief.* Preferably do not go over one page of single-spaced typing, almost never over two pages, plus an outline.

3. *Be professional.* Address the editor by name. Type your letter neatly. Single-space, except between paragraphs. Always include a SASE (self-addressed, stamped envelope). Make sure you have all details correct (spelling of names, dates, sources, facts). Submit only one idea at a time. Also, study the market guides and editorial guidelines before submitting a query, so you are sure the particular market might be interested.

4. *Be at your best.* The query is your sales pitch, your opportunity to make a good first impression on the editor. Write and rewrite it with care. Make it a lively sample of your best writing. Let your enthusiasm for the subject and your concern for excellence shine through your query letter.

  If the editor answers your query with a "sorry, we are not interested," pick the next market on your possibility list and submit a new query. If the editor responds with suggestions for changes in your outline or approach, get ready to oblige him as much as possible. Think of him as a member of your communication team, not an obstacle you must lop off enroute to publication. If he says, "Send us your article on speculation," he is not promising to buy it. He simply wants to see the finished article.

With a go-ahead, the ball is now in your court. Carry through on all the promises you have made. If the editor gives you a deadline, meet it. When this is impossible, work out a reasonable alternative with the editor. But never ignore a deadline. Give the editor every reason to be more than glad that he decided to look twice at you and your manuscript.

ROUGH DRAFT

This is an important danger zone. Watch for the following snares:

1. *Premature Writing.* You may experience a tendency to rush into the writing before you have done adequate research. Some research was necessary before you wrote your query. More may be needed now. Do your homework and resist the temptation to produce a substance-thin manuscript.

2. *Wordiness paranoia.* Some writers, in an effort to avoid too many later revisions, write skimpily in rough draft. They leave out facts and impressions that are vital to an understanding of the story. Do not worry about word limits while writing rough drafts. Get it all down and cut later.

THE COOL-OFF

This is that excruciating period when you lay your precious work in the drawer and restrain yourself from retrieving it to examine it every five minutes. In the heat of excitement over your work being accepted on speculation, resist the temptation to omit this crucial step. Discipline yourself during this time to turn your mind to new ideas and research projects. You may develop some valuable spin-offs from your first project—ideas that were suggested by your research but did not survive the sorting-out process of outlining.

I wrote "Slow Down and Live" to share the important learning that had come to me through a painful experience with overcommitment. As I worked on it, I realized I was not covering all the bases. My deep feelings of frustration toward

WHAT DO I DO WITH MY COMPLETED MANUSCRIPT?

some people who were pushing me toward more involvement finally surfaced in a poem, "Please Let Me Be Me." Later two more poems on the same topic emerged. These were spin-off projects, even though they represented new learning and perspectives that I had gained as I grew through the experience.

REWRITE

Your week is up and you release that magical pile of papers from its dark prison. Now with a renewed vision and objectivity, you begin cutting, rearranging, picking, and polishing. I recommend that you join a critique group that can help you with this stage. Your manuscript may have to pass through several more cooling and rewriting periods before it reaches the point of polished professional finesse that qualifies it for the journey to an editor's desk.

SUBMIT

Once the polishing work is done and you are satisfied that your work is ready for editorial scrutiny, you do three things:

1. *Prepare the manuscript neatly.* Type it, double-spaced, on one side only of good quality 20-pound 8-1/2" x 11" white bond paper. (NEVER USE CORRASABLE BOND PAPER!) Leave a margin of 1–1-1/2" (10–15 spaces) on each side of the page. (See Sample Manuscript Typing Guide on page 213). Keep a copy of your manuscript for your files. Also prepare and fill in a Submission Record Form (see sample form on page 214). Attach this to your manuscript copy, and place it in your work folder along with your accumulated notes related to the manuscript. Add submission information to your market file card (see sample on page 215).

2. *Send the manuscript properly.* Manuscripts of two or three pages may be folded like a letter and mailed in a regular legal-sized envelope. Longer manuscripts should be sent flat in a large manila envelope, with a sheet of cardboard or manila folder to protect them. Always enclose a SASE (may be folded) for the editor to use when returning the manuscript (Yes, it can happen, even to your polished gem!).

MANUSCRIPT TYPING GUIDE

NAME_____
ADDRESS_____
CITY   STATE   ZIP_____
SOCIAL SECURITY NUMBER_____

About 1,000 words A
Rights Submitted

B

1
2
3
4
5
6
7
8
9
TITLE_____ 10
BY_____ 11
NAME_____ 12
13
14
15

Prepare a guide like this one, using 8-1/2" x 11" paper.   16
Place this sheet behind the manuscript sheet in your   17
typewriter so that the numbers show to the right of the   18
manuscript. Use it as a guide to show you where to type   19
and when to stop at the bottom of the sheet. Begin   20
typing text on line 16.   21

Succeeding pages begin with your name in the left-   22
hand corner with the page number in the right corner,   23
on line A. The text begins on line B.   24

WHAT DO I DO WITH MY COMPLETED MANUSCRIPT?

SUBMISSION RECORD FORM _____

TITLE_____WORDS_____

SUBMITTED TO:	DATE SENT	DATE SOLD	PAYMENT	DATE RETURNED	POSTAGE

GROSS PROCEEDS_____

NET PROFIT_____

MARKET FILE CARD_____

ETERNITY MAGAZINE, 1716 Spruce St., Philadelphia PA 19103, Stephen Board, Editor

	Sub.	Ret.
Tunnel Vision	7/29/74	8/16/74
What About Those Unsafe Schools?		
	5/30/75	8/8/75 SOLD $50

Send to only one market at a time, unless you have marked it "Simultaneous Submission" in the upper right-hand corner. (See Glossary.) Send only one manuscript to a market at one submission. The exception to this is poetry. You may send three to five poems at one time. This is called "Multiple Submission."

Affix sufficient first-class postage to both the outer envelope and the SASE. Book manuscripts may be sent by UPS. In this case enclose money for return in a separate letter. Do not use the fourth-class book rate. It is allowable for manuscripts, but is slow and not as well treated. Show your editor that you feel your work is worth top treatment.

3. *Wait patiently for an answer.* Be skeptical of all market-guide promises of prompt replies. Program your mind to anticipate a delay. Do not bug your editor, writing or calling him every few days. Such action will probably encourage him to return your manuscript so he will not be subjected to further hassling. After an unreasonable delay (3–6 months), however, it is proper to write a courteous note inquiring about your manuscript.

WHAT DO I DO WITH MY COMPLETED MANUSCRIPT?

NEXT PROJECT

Now that your first story is in the mail, your mind is free to concentrate on the next idea. As you submerge yourself here, time will pass quickly and one day you will receive an answer from the first editor and exclaim, "Already?"

ACCEPTANCE OR REJECTION

At last the day comes—your inevitable encounter with truth. The postman brings you a sharp, businesslike, legal-sized envelope with the magazine's logo in the upper left-hand corner. Inside you find a letter of acceptance and probably a check. Your joy is complete. You hug the postman, your children, and the dog.

Or the envelope you hold in your hand looks discouragingly familiar. Your SASE is now unfolded and postmarked, bearing the manuscript in company with a form rejection slip (or personal letter, if you are unusually blessed).

If your story is accepted, sit down immediately and write a thank-you note to the editor. This may constitute paragraph one of a new query letter concerning the project you were working on while he evaluated story one. Of course, if the new idea is not right for this same market, send the new query elsewhere. Wherever possible, though, suggest another idea and follow it up. Never let a pleased editor forget you.

If the moment of truth was rejection, take heart. This is recycling time. Pick the next magazine on your list. Type a new query letter (if required) or send the manuscript off this very day. Never let the sun go down on a rejected manuscript.

REJECTION

My manuscript returned today—
  Silent
  Sober
  Slightly dog-eared—
In company with gray rejection slip:
  "Thanks for letting us
    review your work of art;

It doesn't fit
　　our present needs.
Try us again
　　another day."
I'VE BEEN REJECTED!

My spirit's changed 'twixt morn and night.
　From mood of gloom
　again I rise
　　to optimism,
　　as market guide catches my eye.
　Page on page
　　filled with other markets.
I flip them over,
scan them hungrily,
　then pick an address,
　type it out,
　stamp two envelopes.
Expectantly
　I send my brainchild on its way.
　For now I know
　　it was my manuscript
　　the editor returned,
　　　and clearly,
I WAS NOT REJECTED!

PUBLICATION

If you thought the acceptance day was exciting, wait for this one. When you hold in your hand your very first published manuscript and see your name in print, along with those words you labored so hard to produce and polish, the whole world turns to sunshine and a rainbow of colors. If for the next few days you find yourself calling all your friends to invite them over for coffee so you can just happen to show them your new display, or if you set the magazine (opened to the proper page) on your kitchen counter, coffee table, dresser, or mirror—wherever you will see it a hundred times a day—consider yourself normal. But do not allow yourself more than a few spare moments here and there for celebrations. You have more projects to write, and they will not get done while you are giving tea parties to doting friends.

Can you believe me when I tell you this is still *not* the end for your manuscript?

SUBMIT FOR REPRINT

Now begins the process of once more submitting your manuscript to other magazines—this time for reprint rights. You may submit them either as simultaneous submissions to denominational magazines with nonoverlapping readerships or to one magazine at a time.

Your story may not be immortal—at least not quite. Yet it will live on. The words you write today may circle the globe in a suitcase, be read on the radio, find their way into a movie or TV production, be chosen for inclusion in an anthology, and on and on. No matter how old your story grows, the time is never too late to thank God for it—for what it did for you, for the editors who liked it and gave it a distinguished birthing, for each reader whose life has been touched—or ever will be.

Lesson Eleven
Part Two
Rewriting and Polishing the Final Version

Your rough draft has lain tucked away in a drawer for at least a week. Meanwhile you have been filling your mind with new ideas, market studies, query letters, maybe even some research or writing exercises. At last the time has come to rouse your sleeping brainchild and groom him for his long trip to the editor's conference room.

This lesson will lead you through this exacting and sometimes painful process. First, we shall look at the reasons for and mechanical approaches to rewriting. Then we shall examine the Four-Reading Method for rewriting and polishing manuscripts.

IN DEFENSE OF REWRITING

Nothing you write is chiseled in granite. No matter how inspired you felt when you wrote something or how good you thought it was when you wrote *Finis* across the page, it is not sacred, inspired, infallible, and probably not even terribly good. Lest this discourage you, remember that even the pros do not write—they rewrite. One of the signs that a pro is a pro is that he is willing to cut and rewrite as many times as it takes to make his work come out just right.

Rewriting helps us to insure that:
1. We have said what we intended to say.
2. We have made our work believable and understandable.
3. We have made it interesting, smooth, captivating, and significant to our target audience.
4. We have made it marketable.

THE MECHANICS OF REWRITING

What method is best for rewriting? This depends on the writer. Experiment and find the methods that work best for you. Certain things are essential for all rewriting:
1. Write copiously and fully in the rough-draft stage. Leave plenty of room for cutting.
2. Type the rough draft double or triple space, leaving generous margins for ease in penciling in corrections.
3. Do not start revising too soon. Do not shortcut the cooling-off periods.

Other specific approaches differ with the writer and his subject. Here are the standard ones:

Blue Pencil. Mark things out; pencil in revisions, corrections, additions. Incidentally, the pencil need not be blue, and it is best not to use a pen as you may have many occasions to erase. This method can get messy and hard to read, after a time.

Cut and Glue. Cut things out with scissors, and glue them into different spots or eventually discard them. The main problem here is that you may want to put material back in or return it to its original order. This is more difficult to do once you have cut and destroyed. Do not destroy any of your pieces until the process is complete and your manuscript has been purchased for publication. Stapling is less permanent than gluing and hence makes additional changes easier.

Fresh Start. Rewrite by starting over and making changes as you go. At times the momentum gained by retyping facilitates the thinking process. However, this is a time-consuming method.

I use a combination of all the above. Generally, I begin with the blue pencil. When the page gets too full of marks and becomes illegible or confusing, I retype. I seldom resort to the cut-and-paste method, and I like to keep a copy of each draft for future reference. In fact, many whole passages that I have cut from manuscripts fit beautifully into others later on.

Critique Group. This method is generally reserved for the time when you have done all you know to do with your manuscript on your own. Then you take it to your group for objective help.

THE FOUR-READING METHOD

Rewriting and polishing consist of:
1. Cutting superfluous words, sentences, and paragraphs
2. Adding new words, phrases, and ideas
3. Rearranging words, sentences, paragraphs, and ideas
4. Rewording for increased effectiveness
5. Correcting errors of grammar, spelling, punctuation, and word accuracy.

The basis for this method is a series of four complete read-throughs of your manuscript. You may need to repeat one or more of these steps many times before you have a completely satisfactory manuscript.

FIRST READING:

CHECKING FOR INTENT: THE COMMUNICATION DIMENSION
Read your manuscript ALOUD straight through, stopping only to make notes and marks in the margins, for reworking later. As you read, ask these questions:
1. What is my thesis? Can I state it in a sentence?
2. Did I say what I intended to say? (The critique group or an impartial reader can help you with this one.)
3. Is my idea significant? Stimulating? Timely? Practical?
4. Did I narrow my focus sufficiently so that I could cover my thesis adequately? Or did I try to cover too much territory and end up not saying anything well?
5. What is unique or fresh about my slant on the subject?

6. Did I make this manuscript appealing to my target audience? Is my style appropriate (language, mood, depth level)? Are my illustrations geared to the right age, doctrinal, and/or interest group? Do I have the right authority image to reach this audience?

7. Does the form I have chosen for this piece enhance its effectiveness in reaching my target audience? If not, should I change the form? Or should I consider a different audience?

8. Did I meet the editorial requirements of my target publication? Word length? Type of material? Subject matter? Style of writing? Special requirements (taboos, lead types, doctrinal stand)?

Poetry

1. When read aloud, do the words sound good together? Mark words that jolt you or stop the train of thought.

2. Is this poem one I can share with someone else? If so, with whom? How many people could profit from it? Is there a market that uses this type of poetry?

Articles

1. Does it raise unanswered questions? If so, does it suggest a strategy for finding answers?

2. Is it truly an article or is it an essay? A personal experience story? A sermon?

Fiction

1. Is there a believable point or moral to my story? Did I weave the point into my story instead of tacking it onto the end?

2. Does my theme come through clearly?

3. Does it apply to the reader I am aiming for?

4. Does my main character have an important problem or goal? Is it stated clearly and early in the story?

5. Have I placed real obstacles in the path of my main character that keep him from achieving his goal easily?

6. Does he solve the problem or reach the goal satisfactorily himself? (In fiction nothing may just happen.)

7. Does the plot seem realistic or contrived?

SECOND READING:

CHECKING FOR CONTENT: THE ARTISTIC DIMENSION
Read the entire manuscript ALOUD again—this time making some changes as you go. Ask yourself these questions:

1. Are all my statements perfectly clear?
2. Are they honest expressions of my beliefs or of the beliefs of those I have quoted?
3. Are there any inaccuracies or any things I need to check for accuracy (facts, quotations, sources, names, etc.)? Are my ideas and facts adequately documented?
4. Do I offer hope to my reader? Am I fair in my presentation of the issues? Do I ignore sides of an issue that I prefer not to deal with?
5. Have I used colorful word pictures to communicate abstract concepts? Is my dialogue realistic?
6. Have I avoided preachiness? Dullness? Triteness?
7. Is my viewpoint realistic? Are my points practical or are they too theoretical or technical to be of any value?
8. Have I controlled my writing and stayed out of the buttercups?
9. Is everything related to my thesis? Are there whole paragraphs or sections I need to omit?
10. Do I have an arresting beginning? A logically progressing middle? A powerful, punch-packing, memorable ending?
11. Are my transitions clear and effective?
12. Does it read smoothly? Does it drag? Is anything awkward or out of place? Are my ideas in the right order?
13. Have I placed emphasis in the proper places? Have I used short, poignant statements? An element of surpise? Quotes and/or dialogue?

Poetry
1. Does it have a clearly discernible beginning, middle, and ending?
2. Have I avoided sentimentality? Moralizing? Triteness? Fogginess? Inversion? Incohesiveness? Lack of substance?

Articles

1. Does everything in the article fit? Is it relevant?
2. Does my ending fit in with the beginning?
   a. Is it a good summary of the thesis and points?
   b. Does it present an effective challenge?
   c. Does it surprise the reader, yet leave him happy?
3. Does it *show* more than *tell?*

Fiction

1. Do my characters act like real people? Do they have faces? Have I described them physically? Are they unique from each other?
2. Do my characters act consistently with their basic character traits? Do they grow and change during the story?
3. Can my readers sympathize with my main character? Is he likable? Normal? Is he logically and sufficiently motivated for all his actions?
4. Does the main character have one dominant trait that is tied to the story problem and/or its solution?
5. Does my opening reach out and grab the reader?
   Does it introduce my main characters?
   Does it set the scene and mood?
   Does it introduce the problem?
   Does it suggest complications and hint at a solution?
6. Does my opening begin close enough to the "day that is different"?
7. Is my opening too heavily laden with details, descriptions, and background information? Or is it crisp and to the point?
8. Does the action in the body of the story continue to interest the reader? Does the story move right along? Does it build suspense? Are the scenes held together with carry-over features?
9. Does my ending carry a dramatic punch that makes the story memorable?
10. Does my ending tie up all the loose ends? Does it satisfy the reader?
11. Does the ending grow naturally out of the story without being predictable?

12. If I have a surprise ending, did I plant enough clues earlier in the story so that the reader believes my ending?

THIRD READING:

CHECKING FOR DETAILS: THE TECHNICAL DIMENSION

Read the manuscript ALOUD for the third time, picking at it for all those nasty little details that can make the difference between slovenly and masterful work. Ask:

1. Is my style simple or cluttered? Sincere or affected? Appropriate to my subject?
2. Are my paragraphs properly divided? Is there one thought per paragraph?
3. Are my sentences the right length? Are they varied in length? In the right order? All necessary? Written in complete thoughts?
4. Have I used any words too many times? Have I used unnecessary words?
5. Have I made right word choices? Do I have colorful words? Action words? Specific words? Accurate words? Appropriate words? Simple words? Precisely correct words?
6. Have I used clichés?
7. Have I committed errors of grammar? Have I switched pronouns? Switched tenses? Do I have shoddily constructed sentences? Mixed points of view? Uneven parallels? Run-on sentences? Disagreement of subject and verb?
8. Have I committed errors of spelling? Punctuation? Capitalization?
9. Have I relied on dashes, exclamation marks, italics, and quotation marks to do what proper word choices and arrangement should accomplish?

Poetry

1. Have I used imagery? Picture words? Sensory words? Poetic language?
2. If I've used rhyme, is it patterned or unpatterned? If

patterned, is the pattern consistent? Is all my rhyme true rhyme? Does it sound contrived?

3. Do the words and phrases chosen fit the mood, theme, and form of my poem?
4. Have I overpunctuated? Underpunctuated?
5. Have I used an interesting arrangement of lines on the page?

Articles

1. Are my statistics, facts, and/or quotes all accurate?
2. Are my anecdotes crisp, clear, and relevant?

Fiction

1. Is my dialogue frequent? Natural? Does it help to characterize my characters? Move the story forward? Provide essential background knowledge?
2. Are all my flashbacks necessary? Properly placed? Clear? Smooth? The proper length?
3. Have I interwoven descriptions with action, dialogue, and narration?
4. Have I used effective show-and-tell techniques?

FOURTH READING:

CHECKING FOR RESPONSE: THE IMPACT DIMENSION
Give your manuscript to an impartial critic to read. Ask him these questions:

1. Did it interest you? Mildly? Intensely? Unusually?
2. Did it make you feel anything? What?
3. Did it stimulate you to think? Change your mind? Reconsider your ideas?
4. Did it arouse you to do anything? To change any attitudes?
5. Did it simply strengthen the convictions you already held?

As you work over your manuscript and use all these questions, you may sometimes be tempted to toss the whole idea out as a bad dream. DON'T! Stop first and do four things:

1. Review your gifts as a writer.
2. Recognize where you are in the creative cycle.

3. Recall the rewards of becoming a writer.
4. Renew the commitment to "run with patience the race
   . . . looking unto Jesus the author and finisher of our
   faith." (Hebrews 12:2, 3)

On the occasion of one of my major manuscript rejections, as I faced the need to scrap most of my work and start over, my mother wrote the following piece which revived my sagging enthusiasm and sent me on to do the ultimate in rewriting. I share it with you, just in case you feel what you have had to cut and polish may be more painful than it is worth.

THE PARABLE OF THE POMEGRANATE
(For a Very Dear Fruit-Farmer)

My first pomegranate intimidated me. "Delicious," they said. That meant there had to be a way to eat a pomegranate, but I could not find it. The skin was hard, so I could not bite it. If I stuck it, it bled horribly. It was messy, and stained my clothes. But it was beautiful, so I set it on a shelf where I admired it till it shriveled up, cracked, and turned dark. I threw it away.

Then I saw kids eating pomegranates. Fascinated, I watched as they bit and chewed and spit out seeds, all the time clamoring for more. My mouth watered, and I wondered if I dared? . . .

That time I found a way. I broke off a small section and found a compact packet of individual seeds, each wrapped in a magic blanket of juice. The flavor was exotic, irresistible! . . . But . . . those seeds were such a bother. . . .

"Maybe we don't need pomegranates," I said. "We have other delicious, juicy fruits. Pomegranates? Forget them!" Yet, there was something distinctive about their flavor, and I craved it.

Later, I learned how the pomegranate could be pressed into yielding its distinctive essence in the form of juice. And oh, the things you could do with that juice! Jellies, drinks, syrup—with a flavor no other fruit could quite duplicate.

Today I know you don't have to eat a pomegranate. You find a way to make it yield its essence. If you want that essence enough, you take it seed by seed and find it worth the effort. Or you extract its essence and create new forms for it.

But NOTHING can take its place, and . . .

YOU *NEVER, NEVER, NEVER, NEVER* THROW A POME-GRANATE AWAY!

—Alice Funkhouser

ASSIGNMENT:

1. Write a query letter for your personal experience story to the editor of your first choice of market. This is a practice letter. Do not send it until you have completed polishing your story. This is a good procedure to follow with all your stories until you learn to know your own pace and reliability record.
2. Polish your personal experience story. Share it with your critique group if you have one; finish polishing your piece. When it is ready, prepare it according to the format in the lesson; then submit it and go on to another project. See the Appendix for more writing exercises.
3. If you are ready to form a critique group, study the guidelines given in the Appendix.

CONCLUSION

BECOMING THE WRITER I COULD BE

The word *writer* may not call for capital letters, gold plaques, or crystal pedestals to do it justice. As you have plodded through the pages of this book, however, you have spent considerable time learning what it does imply. You also now have an educated appreciation for the high respect such a title deserves.

You and all the other readers of this book entertain visions of writing grandeur that vary widely, along with the kinds of bodies you live in and the temperaments that control you. Some of you are day workers; others, night owls. Some have natural research itches; others are too spontaneous to care about anything so "uncreative." You practice your craft in different ways, in different kinds of environments.

In this final chapter, I want to introduce you to fourteen of my hypothetical writing friends that typify most of the writers you will ever meet. Among these vignettes, you will undoubtedly find yourself mirrored somewhere. I trust that in so doing, you will begin to get some idea of how you can become the best kind of writer you can be.

Shoe-box Slave writes compulsively. Cut off his writing arm, and he is sure he would faint and die. Yet, he takes utmost care never to show one line of his inspired inscriptions to another soul. So they accumulate in write-your-own notebooks with padded covers or on miscellaneous scraps of paper stashed away in shoe boxes.

Prolific Poet is a highly inspired bard who writes volumes of verse. She never changes a word or a comma, for she knows true inspiration needs no improvement. Sensing that her writing is a ministry, she shares her multitude of poems with every friend, acquaintance, and unwary stranger she meets. She basks in the glowing warmth of the praises of all the overawed unknowledgeable recipients of her golden pen jottings. She plans on someday publishing a collection that will give her an immortality to rival that of Shakespeare.

Gold Digger knows there is a fortune to be found in his typewriter and a fame that knows no equal. He consumes books on "How To Get Rich By Writing," studies the bestseller lists and magazine markets and thoroughly exploits every subject he finds by doing a dozen articles and sixteen fillers—all from his research on a single theme. Convinced that writing constitutes the rainbow that will lead to his pot of gold, he quit his job prematurely to go full-time as a free-lancer, and his poor family has been struggling ever since. Sadly, he has not even noticed that little by little he has begun to write from dearth of substance and even compromise some principles in his determined pursuit of fame and fortune.

Ivory Tower Hermit considers himself an expert commentator on the lives of other people. When he is not expounding heavy truths, he buries himself in Bible study and the formulation of theoretical, theologically correct approaches to life's great problems. An important think-tank for the Christian community, he is much too busy studying, theorizing, and solving the world's problems to mix with the world and find out what really goes on there. Further, he fears contact with people and controversy and strives to protect his sure opinions at all cost.

Research Addict lives by the motto "All writers must read widely." The printed page draws her by some mysterious inner magnet so that she dares not leave a source untouched. Who knows what rare gem she might miss if she quits too soon? She resists finishing her research and beginning the writing because (1) she cannot bear the thought of parting with her beloved project, (2) she feels terribly intimidated by the empty page and other writing disciplines, and (3) her artistic nature is repelled by business details.

Perpetual Polisher is never satisfied with a manuscript, as it is. He can always think of ways to improve it. So he goes on polishing and polishing, literally to the death. Since his work never becomes polished enough for publication, even editors do not get a chance to review it.

Idea Genius has a brain that sprouts ideas like a wild mustard field in spring. She can write clever leads and promising query letters. She reads everything with a critical eye and could write helpful book reviews if she got around to it. She might make an excellent agent or a critic or a catalyst for a class on idea mining. But she rarely finishes a manuscript, because long before that point, she has come up with thirteen more ideas that lure her away from her typewriter.

Multi-talented Wonder paints, sings, entertains, teaches, crochets, repairs broken furniture, baby-sits the neighbor's children, runs the Women's Missionary Society *ad infinitum.* She finds it impossible to choose between talents; she might lose some of life's richness that way. For her, to say "NO" is too painful even to contemplate, except when it comes to the call of her dust-collecting IBM Selectric II, which her family gave her on her birthday.

Destiny Writer believes that in every person lies one good story. He spends half a lifetime looking for his story. Finding it, he applies himself with diligence and commendable endurance and writes it. That completed, he sells his typewriter and goes on to greener pastures, with great satisfaction that his literary mission in life has been fulfilled.

Single-mission Prophet is a cousin to Destiny Writer. She feels a godly compulsion to crusade on paper for her one consuming interest. She narrows the scope of her research, reading, and conversation to that one topic. She gets so involved in her "calling" that she develops a lopsided personality and settles down to live in a deep and muddy rut.

Frustrated Dreamer is constantly thwarted in her attempts to write by the uncontrollable constraints of life—young children, a husband, a career, the inability to find a satisfactory focus for her ideas. At times the imaginary enemies bombard her as well—lack of inspiration, time, encouragement, and talent. Misplaced priorities further frustrate her. The one thing she always finds time for is to talk about her frustrations to anyone who will give her a hearing.

Shaky Procrastinator lives next door to Frustrated Dreamer. Over cups of herb tea, they make constant plans for the great literary works they will produce. She is always waiting for something to happen so she can make her break into print. First the children must grow up, the house must be finished, inspiration must strike, good ideas must come along; she must get rid of some tensions, and the Lord must give her a clear call. Someday the world will be shaken to its axis by her literary prowess—but not yet. There's too much left to be done first.

Literary Worshiper has a hankering to write. He reads much and dreams of writing. Because he enjoys the company of published writers, he joins writers' clubs, takes writing classes, and attends writers' conferences. However, writing takes a level of discipline and organization that are foreign to him. He cannot take criticism for the few things he ventures to produce and share with a critique group. But the fact that he is a writer you can easily discern—*just ask him!*

Editor's Delight is that rare well-disciplined person who has managed to put his whole life in balance. He identifies the bothersome traits he shares in common with his fellow-writers (or would-be writers) listed above, and works to overcome each hindrance. He studies writing, human nature, and theology, along with a host of other fascinating and practical subjects. Then he goes on to translate his thoughts into manuscripts. He joins a critique group and uses it constructively. A consistent Christian and student of the Scriptures, he majors on staying sensitive to the leading of the Holy Spirit. He also learns to work with people and relate to and learn from them. He is a self-assured, confident worker and minister who consistently produces and sells good quality, significant healing literature for the broken persons in the Body of Christ.

In his attempt to progress past the point where he started in one of the first thirteen categories, *Editor's Delight* found three keys to open the doors for his coveted position: (1) disciplined craftsmanship, (2) balanced living, and (3) sensitivity to his own growth potential, the needs of others, and the will of God.

As you launch yourself on a writing ministry/career, take these same three keys. Insert them in the locks of the doors that stand before you. You, too, will find your place, and whether your identity will ever be Editor's Delight or not, at least you can achieve the prize title of all, carved in gold, with capital letters, and mounted on a crystal pedestal: GOD'S DELIGHT.

ASSIGNMENT:

Answer the following questions:
1. What have I gained of most benefit from this course?
2. How have my goals changed?
3. How do I feel, now, about my gift as a writer?
4. What specific steps do I plan to take next?

BOOKS FOR WRITERS

RECOMMENDED READING

PERSONAL PREPARATION

Alexander, John W. *Practical Criticism*. Downers Grove IL: InterVarsity Press, 1976. Small booklet

L'Engle, Madeleine. *A Circle of Quiet*. New York: Farrar, Straus and Giroux, Inc., 1972. A writer writes about her life and writing

Lewis, C. S. *Mere Christianity*. New York: Macmillan Publishing Co., Inc., 1943. Classic apologetic

Mitson, Eileen. *Reaching for God*. Chappaqua NY: Christian Herald, 1978. Autobiography of deep-thinking British writer

Ogilvie, Lloyd John. *The Autobiography of God*. Ventura CA: Regal, 1979. Fascinating exposition of the parables of Christ.

Packer, J. I. *Knowing God*. Downers Grove IL: InterVarsity Press, 1973. Must reading for every Christian

Rookmaaker, Hans. *Art Needs No Justification*. Downers Grove IL: InterVarsity Press, 1978. Christian philosophy of art

Ryken, Leland. *Literature of the Bible*. Grand Rapids MI: Zondervan Publishing House, 1974. Excellent and practical

————. *Triumphs of the Imagination*. Downers Grove IL: InterVarsity Press, 1979. Literature in the life of Christians

Schaeffer, Francis. *Art and the Bible*. Downers Grove IL: InterVarsity Press, 1973. Insightful Christian perspective

Sire, James W. *How to Read Slowly*. Downers Grove IL: InterVarsity Press, 1978.

Tournier, Paul. *The Adventure of Living*. New York: Harper & Row Publishers, Inc., 1965. Great pointers on coping with life as a Christian

White, John. *The Fight*. Downers Grove IL: InterVarsity Press, 1976. Great clichéless writing

GRAMMAR AND STYLE

Flesch, Rudolph, and Lass, S. H. *A New Guide to Better Writing*. New York: Popular Library, 1963 (Paperback). Hardback title—*The Way to Write*. New York: Harper & Row Publishers, Inc., 1949.

Strunk, William, Jr. *The Elements of Style*. New York: Macmillan Publishing Co., 1959.

Venolia, Jan. *Write Right!* Woodland Hills CA: Periwinkle Press, 1979. Great handy desk guide

Zinsser, William. *On Writing Well*. New York: Harper & Row Publishers, Inc., 1976.

GENERAL WRITING TECHNIQUES

Anderson, Margaret J. *The Christian Writer's Handbook.* New York: Harper & Row Publishers, Inc., 1974.

Bell, Donald, and Merrill, John C. *Dimensions of Christian Writing.* Grand Rapids: Zondervan Publishing House, 1970. Out of print and heavy reading, but well worth the effort

Flesch, Rudolph. *The Art of Readable Writing.* New York: Harper & Row Publishers, Inc., 1949.

Perrine, Laurence. *Literature, Structure, Sound, and Sense.* New York: Harcourt Brace & Jovanovich, 1974. Excellent literature textbook covering many details of writing technique

The Writer. 8 Arlington St., Boston MA 02116. Excellent and practical magazine

WRITING ARTICLES AND NON-FICTION BOOKS

Holmes, Marjorie. *Writing the Creative Article.* Boston: The Writer, 1969.

Gunther, Max. *Writing and Selling the Non-Fiction Book.* Boston: The Writer, 1973.

————. *Writing the Modern Magazine Article.* Boston: The Writer, 1973.

WRITING POETRY

Berg, Viola. *Pathways for the Poet.* Milford MI: Mott Media, 1977.

Hardy, Elizabeth Stanton. *Poetry: The Shaping of Words.* New York: Bookman Associates, 1956. Out of print

Ciardi, John, and Williams, Miller. *How Does A Poem Mean?* Boston: Houghton Mifflin Co., 1975.

WRITING BIOGRAPHY

Bowen, Catherine Drinker. *Biography: The Craft and the Calling.* Westport CT: Greenwood Press, 1978.

WRITING FOR CHILDREN

Wyndham, Lee. *Writing for Children and Teenagers.* Cincinnati: Writer's Digest, 1968.

WRITING HISTORY

Cairns, Earle E. *God and Man in Time.* Grand Rapids MI: Baker Book House, 1979.

Gottschalk, Louis. *Understanding History.* New York: Alfred A. Knopf, 1961.

SUGGESTED REFERENCE BOOKS

ESSENTIAL BOOKS (based on my own preferences)

Dictionary:
American Heritage Dictionary of the English Language.

Synonym Dictionary:
Roget's Thesaurus. An Alphabetically indexed edition is best.

Bible Concordances:
Strong's Exhaustive Concordance of the Bible; Young's Exhaustive Concordance
is also good.

Bible Handbook:
Eerdmans Handbook to the Bible by David and Patricia Alexander. Grand
    Rapids MI: Wm. B. Eerdmans Publishing Co., 1973.

Grammar and Technical Points:
Write Right! by Jan Venolia. Woodland Hills CA: Periwinkle Press, 1980.

A New Guide to Better Writing by Rudolph Flesch & A. H. Lass. New York:
    Popular Library, 1963.

Market Guide:
The Writer's Market published by Writer's Digest and updated every year.

The Religious Writer's Marketplace by William H. Gentz & Elaine Wright
    Colvin. Philadelphia: Running Press, 1980.

Manuscript Preparation:
Preparing the Manuscript by Udia Olsen. The Writer.

GREAT-TO-HAVE BOOKS

Usage dictionaries

Literary dictionaries

Rhyming dictionaries

Almanac

Law and the Writer by Kirk Polking. (Cincinnati: Writer's Digest, 1978.)

A Treasury of Tips for Writers by Marvin Weisbord. (Cincinnati: Writer's
    Digest, 1965.)

SPECIALIZED BOOKS

Bible Dictionaries:
The New Bible Dictionary by J. D. Douglas. Grand Rapids MI: Wm. B. Eerdmans
    Publishing Co., 1962.

The Illustrated Bible Dictionary (3 vols.) Wheaton IL: Tyndale House Pub-
    lishers, Inc., 1981. Revised, expanded, and illustrated version of *The New
    Bible Dictionary.*

Bible Encyclopedias:

The Zondervan Pictorial Encyclopedia of the Bible (5 vols.) Edited by Merrill Tenney. Grand Rapids MI: Zondervan Publishing House, 1975.

The Wycliffe Bible Encyclopedia by Pfeiffer, Vos, and Read. Chicago: Moody Press, 1975.

Topical Bible Handbooks:

Nave's Topical Bible by Orville J. Nave. Chicago: Moody Press, 1975.

Nave's Topical Living Bible by Orville J. Nave. Wheaton IL: Tyndale House Publishers, Inc., 1982.

The New Compact Topical Bible by Gary Wharton. Grand Rapids MI: Zondervan Publishing House, 1972.

Bible Customs:

Manners and Customs by James Freeman. Plainfield NJ: Logos International, 1972.

Manners and Customs by Fred Wight. Chicago: Moody Press, 1953.

Strange Scriptures That Perplex the Western Mind by Barbara M. Bowen. Grand Rapids MI: Wm. B. Eerdmans Publishing Co., 1944.

Bible Introductions:

Exploring the Scriptures by John Phillips. Chicago: Moody Press, 1965.

Atlases:

The Macmillan Bible Atlas by Yohanan Aharoni and Michael Avi-Yonah. New York: Macmillan Publishing Co., Inc., 1968.

The Macmillan Atlas History of Christianity by Franklin H. Littell. New York: Macmillan Publishing Co., Inc., 1976.

REPRINTS FROM ARTICLES BY ETHEL HERR

Is There a Camel in Your Tent?

At 4:30 on a grayish Sunday afternoon, Dick and Marcia sat down to a cup of strong coffee. Dick yawned. Marcia stared into her steaming handcrafted mug.

"Dick, I'm afraid there's a camel in our tent again," she announced.

Dick looked puzzled. "What tent? What camel? What are you talking about?" he asked.

Still staring into her coffee, Marcia went on: "Don't you remember the story of the Arab and the camel? The camel came to the Arab and begged, 'Please let me warm my nose in your tent.'"

Dick spoke up, "Yeah, I remember. The Arab opened his tent flap and let the camel's nose in. Next thing he knew, here came the forelegs, the hump, the tail . . ."

"Until he completely occupied the tent," Marcia finished.

"So?" Dick gulped down the last of his coffee, grabbed his Bible and headed for the door, shouting, "Come on kids! Time to run. Youth groups start in ten minutes."

Enroute to church, Marcia decided to approach the subject head on. "Remember when we moved here? We didn't tell a soul we could teach a Bible lesson or sing in the choir or even address an envelope."

"Um-hm," Dick muttered, as he shrieked to an impatient halt before a red light.

"We were so naive we thought we could keep people from knowing how our talents had practically run the church we came from," Marcia added a bit sarcastically.

"For a whole year you didn't do a thing at church," thirteen-year-old Jane offered from the back seat.

"Yeah, we used to sit together for every service," said ten-year-old Bill. "It was neat!"

Dick ran his fingers through his thinning hair. "Then how

did we manage to get so involved? Here we are Sunday school teachers, junior church leaders, bus driver, orchestra director, junior high youth sponsors, C. E. board members . . ."

Marcia sighed. "There's where the camel comes in. It all started the week I counselled at camp. Remember? That was the camel's nose. During the week, somebody discovered we had a few talents. Then one by one, we let people talk us into a dozen responsibilities."

"Aha," Dick said. "So that's how the sanctified talent camel has come once more to occupy our family tent. I think you may be right."

Dick and Marcia never intended to overcommit themselves. But they loved the Lord, wanted to serve him, and had listened to a lot of sermons on the parable of the talents. Once they identified the problem, they did some hard figuring and praying about priorities. Then they marched off to the powers that sat in the church office, and handed in a few long-overdue resignations. They finally learned that talents are a gift from God. But in his master plan, he's allotted both a time and a place for each one. Rarely does he choose to use every talent at once and with the same degree of intensity.

The twentieth-century church is full of Dicks and Marcias. Many of us reach a point where we feel like the junior high boy I knew. His father insisted that he join the youth choir. When the boy objected, his father would say, "But son, this is a golden opportunity the Lord has given you to develop your talent and serve." One day the boy countered his father's reminder with a bit of desperate honesty: "Well, I just wish the Lord would stop piling on the golden opportunities."

Today's multi-talented Christian faces a dilemma. In most churches he's victimized by a strange inconsistency. If a brother (or sister) complains: "I don't have any talents," we pat him on the back and assure him God has given him some sort of gifts. We even pray for him and perhaps scare up some little thing he can do.

If however, he contends: "Look I just can't do another thing," we show little sympathy. Instead we admonish him: "But you're so talented; just the man the Lord has called to this ministry."

The whole situation seems to me to have evolved from our

acceptance of six convincing myths about talents and Christian service.

First is the myth that church activity is always service. If we are active in church work, we are "obviously" serving the Lord. And if we want to serve the Lord, we must "obviously" get ourselves involved up to the eyeballs in *church* work.

The result is that many Christians resemble a child on a coin-operated horse at the supermarket. As long as the coin holds out, they go like crazy, generating tremendous activity. But they don't get anywhere. When the coin runs out, they're still sitting where they started.

The Apostle Peter must have encountered this problem back in the first century. That's why he wrote in I Peter 4:8-11: "As each one has received a special gift, employ it in serving one another, as good stewards of the manifold grace of God. Whoever speaks, let him speak as it were, the utterances of God; whoever serves, let him do so as by the strength which God supplies."

While activity is not always wrong, it is not necessarily service to God. Obedience to individual guidance, on the other hand, will always be a service to Jesus Christ. This may take the form of ringing doorbells for the Heart Fund or local school bond issue. It may mean sitting very still to worship, or simply enjoying a bicycle ride, a sunset or a jigsaw puzzle. Our first service to God is to become all he wants us to become, letting him form in us his own image, for the *world* (not just our church co-workers) to see.

A second myth states that having a talent gives us the automatic responsibility to use and develop that talent to the fullest possible extent.

A young woman told me of her sister who "has a dozen talents, and she's convinced she has a duty to fully develop every one. But the strain of trying to keep up with such a program is killing her."

Talents are the tools the master Artist uses to sculpture character and spiritual excellence in us. Our service is not half so important to him as our dedication and sensitivity to his person.

God's will is not always externally obvious. But it is always discernible. Many things figure into God's plan for us. Things

242

like our own personal growth, the community where we live, current social trends and many more. As we learn to focus on God intimately, we can discover which talents he's scheduled for development today.

Which leads to a third myth: that God calls to a specific job, and his calling is for a lifetime.

I once had a friend whose son served as a church minister of music. When the church phased out his position, he decided to teach music in the public school and continue to serve churches on a part-time basis.

My friend objected: "God called this boy to be a minister of music, not a schoolteacher."

God had not called her boy to a job or even to a ministry. God had called this young man to himself, a calling which could involve many changes of occupation and ministry along the way.

This is the thrust of Romans 12:1, 2. "With eyes wide open to the mercies of God, I beg you, my brothers, as an act of intelligent worship, to give him your bodies, as a living sacrifice, consecrated to him and acceptable by him. Don't let the world around you squeeze you into its own mold, but let God remold your minds from within, so that you may prove in practice that the plan of God for you is good, meets all his demands, and moves toward the goal of true maturity." (J. B. Phillips)

If we present our bodies as a daily sacrifice to God and allow him to remold our minds, he will guide us by his Spirit, in ways sometimes quite foreign to the human logic processes.

A fourth myth hits us all at a vulnerable point. It is the God-will-give-you-strength-to-do-anything argument. One pastor put it this way: "I get the feeling that our evangelical culture has conditioned us quite well to conclude that 'God who is our refuge and strength' will provide the strength to run ourselves to a frazzle."

God gives us strength for those things he designs for us to do. If we are running out of energy, we need to evaluate ourselves, our dreams and our schedules. Let's weed out the God-wants-me-to's from the I'd-surely-love-to's.

The fifth myth feeds an ever-hungry ego. It says that if I don't do a thing, it won't get done—at least not done right.

Two things result from this misconception. First, the talented persons become overcommitted. Secondly, many people with few talents never find a place of usefulness. They can't, until the many-talented persons step down and give them a chance to be discovered.

Church programs stand in constant danger of getting so elaborate and so numerous, so far out of touch with the Holy Spirit, that God refuses to identify himself with them. When approached about doing a job, we may forget or fear to ask, Is this a part of the Lord's guidance for me today? Or is it a place for that quiet, uninvolved brother? Perhaps it's just another *good* idea, not inspired by God at all, but concocted by some human mind?

After many painful experiences with overcommitment, I've concluded that if in reality there is no one to do a job, maybe it doesn't need to be done. At any rate, I'm not responsible to do the whole work of the Body of Christ, not even in my local church.

Finally there is the prevalent little myth that to have too many talents is easier to handle than not to have any.

Have you ever experienced the pains of spreading yourself too thin, while using every talent? Have you known the frustration of trying to pick and choose among a dozen delightful talent options, all of which match your qualifications and interests precisely? Then you know that this myth just isn't so! Having too many talents can pose just as many problems as having no talents—sometimes even more.

All six of these myths contain an element of truth, which makes them believable. Because they are so subtle, we need to maintain a constant watchful attitude against them all. How best to accomplish this?

I think one youth pastor had the idea, when he told his congregation: "God gives to each local church all the human resources needed for maintenance and growth of that body of believers. If each of us will be careful to take our orders from our Head, and encourage one another to do the same, the job will get done. And no one will die of exhaustion, either."

So simple! More occupation with the person of Jesus Christ and less with his service, leads to more love for Jesus Christ. When once we fall in love with him, nothing can stop us from doing his bidding and his service, according to his schedule!

Could this be God's solution to the problem of our modern Dicks and Marcias—the problem of the sly talent camel in our tents?

Reprinted by permission of ETERNITY Magazine, Copyright 1977, Evangelical Ministries, Inc., 1716 Spruce Street, Philadelphia PA 19103.

Assignment at Sunset

Cool bay breezes were just beginning to stir the air around us on that hot July evening. From my chaise lounge on the patio, I heard the telephone ring. Reluctant to be disturbed, I groaned, then made my way into an overly warm house.

"Ethel," a familiar voice came through the receiver, "I had to call you. It's been a dreadful day. I feel like I've been walking a tightrope and finally fell off."

My distressed friend fell silent and I waited. Sometimes she'd open up and talk freely. Like last night, when she'd gone on for an hour about her teenage boys' problems . . . about her parents and their intrusion into her personal affairs . . . about her schooling. . . .

Most often, though, conversation was next to impossible, especially on the telephone. She was like a disturbed child—needing consolation but fearful to reach out for it, hesitant to receive it.

"Was today worse than yesterday?" I asked lamely.

"Much worse," followed by more helpless silence.

Dear Lord, I breathed a prayer. *What do I do now?*

Then it came to me. Tonight I had to transcend the telegap some way.

"Would you like to go for a ride?" I suggested.

"Oh, please take me," the tired voice begged.

I grabbed my purse and Bible. Rushing out the door, I explained my mission to the family and asked, "Please pray for me. This is a rough assignment. I've no idea what to expect, or what I'm going to say."

Lord, where shall I take her? I prayed as I circled the block. *Show me how to relate. Help her to loosen up, maybe even cry a little and let me show her Your love.*

She was waiting on the curb, a pathetic combination of eagerness and timidity. As we headed eastward out of our housing area, I glanced at the dry mountain range ahead, rosy pink in the setting sun.

"Have you ever been up in those hills?" I asked.

"No, I haven't the slightest idea how to get there."

Thank You, Father, at least You've told me which way to go.

We started toward the pink hills, and my friend began to open her heart to me. Relaxation replaced the impersonal tension of the telephone.

At each new turn of the winding road, we found something new to delight us—a park pond filled with big white geese and little brown ducks, a doe with her fawn grazing among roadside weeds. In between scenic wonders, my companion shared her problems.

The situation seemed just made for this woman. For years she'd battled physical and emotional problems, and was incapable of sustaining conversation on a single topic.

The sun was fully set when we started for home. And the evening's beauty was climaxed at a vista point where we looked far out over the valley to another range of mountains that meets the ocean. The mountains were a fiery red against the sky. In the foreground lay the marshlands and salt flats of the San Francisco Bay. They shimmered pink, gold, and red in the setting sun.

We rode on in silence for a while. Then suddenly the hills were behind us, and we passed through the dusky city streets.

"And how do you feel now?" I asked the woman beside me.

"Ever so much better, thank you!" she answered.

Minutes later we sat in her kitchen, deserted by the boys who'd gone out to play ball. We drank some coffee, shared a few verses of Scripture, and a time of prayer.

"I think I can face tomorrow, now," she said. I left her looking much more at ease than when I'd picked her up earlier.

At home, my daughter asked: "Well, how did the rough assignment go, Mom?"

"What rough assignment?" I countered. "It was magnificent!"

I realized that all my own day's heat and fatigue had disappeared in the glory of one sunset, shared with a friend in need.

Reprinted from *Woman's Touch*, Jan/Feb 1978.

Slow Down and Live

"Dear God, even an ulcer might be better than this." My prayer was desperate as I stared at the frustration-circled eyes in my mirror.

Convinced I couldn't face another day, I added, "At least I'd get some rest that way."

The trouble had begun a year earlier when my husband Wally and I started our own part-time business. It had been such a lovely dream. We'd meet new people, learn new things, work *together.*

The dream soon turned into a nightmare though, as Wally's regular work duties increased and the load fell more and more on me. While business was not my first love, I determined to make a success of it.

The work was really rather pleasant, but it took all my time and sapped the creative strength I needed for my family of three school-aged children.

Other things stood in the threatening line as well, such as a host of church responsibilities, plus parent volunteer work at the school.

As the weeks dragged me along, I became almost impossible to live with. I nagged at my husband and children, and at the cross of an eye, I would burst into meaningless tears. Worst of all, prayer became increasingly difficult. God seemed like a stranger.

What lay ahead? I worried. *A nervous breakdown? A divorce? Or maybe an ulcer?* Come to think of it, I'd experienced some strange stomach pains recently.

"Lord," I prayed that morning before my mirror, "don't let it really be an ulcer; but something just bad enough for an excuse to ditch this business and say 'no' to a lot of demanding people."

I had reached the end of myself, but God was ready to take over. Wally received a pay raise equal in value to my average business income. The doctor diagnosed my pains as a nervous stomach, prescribing four daily doses of medicine, a bland diet, and lots of rest.

At first it was hard to stay home nights and take long afternoon rests, but the results were relaxing and beautiful. My family and I got reacquainted—and most important, God and I found each other again.

Two years later, new pressure situations still tempt me to do more than I can, but my keen memories help me to keep things in order. In the process, I have developed what I call my "Guidelines for Emotional Survival." They could be helpful to others:

First, set your priorities. Ask yourself what things are really important to you and your family today.

Secondly, get to know yourself. Set realistic goals that fit into God's plan for you—not your neighbor! Don't expect more of yourself than God does.

Third, learn to say "NO!" Don't worry when Mrs. Do-it-all doesn't understand. If there is no one else to do the job, maybe it doesn't need to be done. In any case, you're not responsible for the whole world's needs.

Fourth, live decisively. Nothing kills more painfully than indecision. At the same time, allow elbow room in your life for changes and discoveries of the new and exciting elements God wants to introduce to you.

Finally, rest. Inactivity is not necessarily time wasted. Take time out. Prop your feet and read a little. Meditate a little on life's simple beauties or profound issues; snooze a little; pray a little; and become intimate with God. Ask him often to keep you unhurried, even on those unavoidable packed-full days.

Today I'm excited about life—not threatened by it. And to keep it running smoothly, I often think about the Great Physician's personal prescription for preventing frustration—and ulcers:

"Be still and know that I am God . . . They that wait upon the Lord shall exchange their strength for his."

First published in *Scope* 1974, Augsburg Publishing House.

APPENDIX ONE

Rags and a Wordless Prayer

Did you ever reach desperation circle?

Not desperation *point*—that point of no advance and no return. But desperation *circle*—where you buzz around and around in your disappointing life, certain there is a way to the light of serenity, but the longer you seek the more frantic you become, and you always end up in the same spot—defeated!

As a young wife I lived in desperation circle for nearly three years.

Geographically my address was Nassaulaan 52, Baarn, The Netherlands. The house was monstrous, and my first winter was an experience in the endurance of young parenthood. Europe's worst winter in 50 years! My California blood guessed it before the newspaper reported it.

Learning to cook on coal heaters to avoid a deep-freeze kitchen; climbing endless stairs (the house had three stories) and kneeling over a bathtub to keep two babies supplied with diapers; pouring $50 worth of smelly coal into greedy stoves every two weeks to heat a 15-foot-high living room ceiling—I tried to take these in my stride.

But as the days grew grayer, domestic pressures mounted. I was sick of a life horizoned by four dark walls, dingy green draperies and three exasperating preschoolers. My patience wore thin, and verbal explosions came more and more frequently.

At first I prayed about it earnestly, then frantically—until I lost the peace of God, even in prayer.

One day, near winter's end, I reached a crisis. The living room floor was cluttered with toys. Heaps of this and that lay on the table. Diapers hung gloomily above the door. In the middle of the shabby floor my three toddlers fought incessantly.

For what seemed the hundredth time that day, I exploded with a flood of harsh scoldings. Then, feeling the pangs of remorse, I cried, "Oh, Lord, what is the matter with me? I was the girl who never got angry with *anyone!* Now, here I am spouting more verbal poison in a month than I have produced in my 25 years."

Desperation turned to humiliation. "Lord, I've prayed about

this dozens of times, and *You just haven't answered!* Please show me the solution and lead me out of this mess. I'll share that solution with every woman on the face of the earth!"

Though I didn't realize it, those months of failure came in answer to a strange prayer of about a year earlier. It had been one night while I was in the hospital to deliver my third baby. The Christian duty nurse was sharing her testimony with me.

"Each time I read my Bible," she had said, "I find something fresh and thrilling in it."

God jolted me with those words of hers. " ...*something fresh and thrilling!* ..." I had been a Christian for 20 years, taught Sunday school since I was nine, even attended a Bible institute. I loved the Bible and read it daily. But in that moment of truth, I knew I did not share my nurse's experience. The yearning of my heart to recapture the freshness of God's Word in daily life, constituted a sort of wordless prayer.

For years I had taught that *"the way up is down."* Now I was to learn the meaning of that axiom. For the next two years I went through that painful process of self-revelation.

Trying to help God answer my prayer, I began rising at five o'clock each morning to study and pray—only to fall asleep on my knees. I took a Sunday school teaching position and other Christian service responsibilities. There were days when I felt I had found an answer, only to fall again into failure and guilt.

One day in June a traveling Bible teacher, named Chrys, came from Greece to stay in our home all summer. Chrys returned often during the next two years, to teach our American Bible study group. He taught deep truths about surrender and abiding in the Lord. I listened with interest, but inwardly rebelled at some of the extremes he suggested.

The following summer, when we studied Romans 6-8, something clicked. I learned that ever since my conversion I was rightly under the management of Jesus Christ. Satan had no more power over me except what I allowed him as I struggled to meet his temptations in my own strength. But, as Chrys insisted, I didn't have to fret over failure. Instead I could confess and forsake my sin in *Christ's* strength. I had only to recognize Satan as the defeated enemy and yield myself to the new Master of my life.

It all sounded lovely—*but!* I was too proud to admit my need, for I didn't yet know how rotten I was. So the Lord opened my heart and showed me a host of resentments and improper thoughts—sinful attitudes which I had been certain I was incapable of.

Not liking what I saw, but not sure how to correct it, I looked to Chrys. I felt that he lived closer to the Lord than I. Little by little I let him dictate my attitude and actions. Frustration resulted until I woke up to the fact that I had become a slave—not to Jesus Christ, but to Chrys. My *Christianity* had become *Chrys*tianity.

That was a dreadful summer. And glorious too! In the midst of my struggles the Lord was stripping from me the ugly rags of self-sufficiency.

Back in my home church, I had sung solos frequently. Here in Baarn, however, the Lord prevented me from even joining the chapel choir. Instead I led singing for a group of junior high youths who couldn't carry a tune. Their songs were out of my range, and my voice began to crack.

"Lord, You have ruined my voice," I complained one night.

He reminded me, "It is *My* voice, and this is the way I choose to use it."

One day I prayed, "God, You have taken so much from me, I hardly recognize myself. But I *am* still a good Sunday school teacher." The next Sunday, though I went to my class well prepared, I stumbled through the whole session. I decided it was just not my day. But when the incident repeated itself week after week, I finally saw the situation for what it was—a heavenly Father's loving removal of one more aspect of my false self-sufficiency.

Self-revelation was followed by the most irresistible unveiling of Jesus Christ I had known. My character, my talents, my plans lay in a stinking heap at my feet. There was nothing left but the overpowering loveliness of my Savior. I fell in love with *Him*—not with the fringe benefits of being His, or with my service for Him.

Now I understood Galatians 2:20: "I am crucified with Christ; nevertheless I live: yet not I, but *Christ liveth in me.*" I saw that Jesus does not seek somebodies. He seeks out nobodies and possesses them as the person through which He communicates Himself.

Remember that prayer of mine back in the hospital? Now, with my erroneous notions destroyed, I had the answer. The Bible sprang to life. I gave the Lord my active will. My Sunday school teaching took on a new dimension. Genuinely excited, I shared things I was *learning*. I even joined the choir, with a restored voice and a new reason for singing.

In my home I found a new kind of victory, the kind of victory that refuses to wallow in the oozy mud of guilt. The kind that receives generous helpings of the wisdom and character of Jesus Christ as a benefit accompanying salvation.

In the five years that have followed, I have learned the need for constant self-revelation and attendant worship. I never share a Bible truth or sing a solo without a burning heart. But the words and notes do not come as easily as they once did. Often I stumble, as a reminder that my usefulness was won by Jesus Christ in a battle at desperation circle.

First printed in *Today*, March 18, 1973 issue.

Then Came Christmas

Christmas Eve was never like this before. I pulled the heavy old draperies aside and looked through frosted window doors. Beyond the second-story balcony lay fog so thick that only an occasional blob of diffused light hinted at the presence of street lamps.

The world outside matched my mood inside: gray, blurred, hard to understand.

From the bed behind me came a painful groan. "Honey, I hurt again," my husband, Wally, said. "Please go to the dispensary and get some more medicine."

Turning to face him, I countered, "That'd be suicide tonight. The fog is worse than pea soup."

It was strange that the idea about fog being like pea soup never meant much before we moved to the Netherlands two years earlier. Wally had always insisted that soup wasn't soup unless it dripped from his spoon like water. Every bowl of pea soup I had ever made had to be three-quarters milk.

But Dutch pea soup fit the fog class. I bought it at the butcher shop. It was frozen in a round white liter carton, printed with blue delft tiles. We almost ate it with a fork, and Wally refused to call it soup.

"Dear, this fog is like the butcher's pea soup," I explained.

"Then let me try a couple of aspirins," he said.

"By morning the fog should be lifted," I suggested, "so I can find the Air Force base and get your medicine."

What a way to spend Christmas day, I thought as I went for a glass of water and the aspirins. This whole season had been out of keeping with my ideas of a holiday, ever since a week ago when we had waited three hours for an overdue airplane at Schiphol International Airport.

Wally's missionary brother and his wife were arriving from Nigeria en route to America for furlough. When they came, we had twenty-four hours together and made the most of the short time. Wally played tour guide all over the little country. He was in and out of our small car in an icy wind that blew off the North Sea with merciless strength. All this time he had a stomachache that grew increasingly worse.

Tour duty over, we returned our relatives to the airport. As the plane took off, a few snowflakes began tossing around.

"Maybe we'll have a white Christmas," I mused. "It would be our first."

"Don't count on it." Wally was always practical. By the time we reached home, the white fairy gymnasts had retreated behind gray cloud curtains above us.

"I think I'm going to die," Wally mumbled feebly when at last he was home again and seated by the fire. He closed his eyes and leaned his head back against the brick mantelpiece. Stepping forward and laying a hand on his forehead, I looked, then blinked, then gasped: "Honey, *you've* got the chicken pox!"

Martha, our kindergartner, had brought the disease home from school. While we were at the airport picking up our family, the two younger children had popped out with them, too.

"It's impossible," I exclaimed. "Surely you had them when

you were growing up. Number seven of eight children, you
wouldn't miss them!"

But the evidence was painfully clear, as quickly the pox
spread over his entire body, from head to toe. His mouth was
lined with them, and they continued down all the way to his
stomach.

The days that followed were a jumble. Medicines to ad-
minister, hot showers and calamine lotion applications to
supervise, special dietetic kitchen duties (jello and bouillon
cubes by the case), entertaining little people that itched. I discovered an ingenious use for my wringer washing machine.
When your only bathtub is the nine-inch deep floor of a
shower, nothing's handier than an old Maytag for soaking
toddlers' red bubbly skins.

House guests further complicated the situation. A young
airman who worked with my husband had invited his girl
friend to spend the Christmas holidays in Holland. Our house
was the *hotel* he chose for her stay. Absorbed as the two young
lovers were in each other, they did very little to contribute to
the smooth operation of the household, though they constantly assured me of their sympathy.

Many nights before climbing the long flight of narrow,
twisting stairs to my room, I helplessly nodded at the mountain of dirty dishes beside the kitchen sink. "You'll just have
to wait until morning," I would mumble.

Trying to put a Christmas together under such circumstances had been a major project. Gift packages had been sent
on their way stateside in October, and the children had
worked weeks in advance to create their little gifts. But there
were many other last-week things I always loved to do: baking
and special decorating, hours of sitting and watching the tree
lights with my husband, times of prayer and meditation to
prepare my heart. This year, there had been no opportunity
for any of these extras.

Come Christmas Eve, however, the gloom began to lift. Our
little ones were just about themselves again. Wally, with a
week's growth of red beard, joined the family festivities. "Pain
or no pain, I wouldn't miss it," he insisted.

Along with our young guests, we managed that evening to
ignore the complications of the past week and celebrate to-

gether. I told the Christmas story, and we all sang carols and spent a few minutes in prayer. Then our airman friend handed out the gifts, and things were almost normal.

Several hours later I lay beside my husband, tired but wide awake. The aspirin had finally done its job, and Wally slept peacefully. But I couldn't.

"Lord," I prayed, "this week's been pretty rough, but tonight was lovely. I'm sorry I've complained. Please help me to make tomorrow pleasant for my poor sick husband."

I must have dozed off to sleep about then. The next thing I knew, Wally was tossing beside me.

"Dear," he moaned, "the pain is awful. You have to get that medicine."

Jumping up, I grabbed my robe and ran to the window. "Let's see how the fog's doing," I offered sleepily.

Nothing that night had prepared me for what I saw as I drew back the draperies this time. Fog? No, not a trace. But pouring down from the sky in soft stealthy gracefulness, was the full cast of fairy snowflakes. Our world was enchanted, as only a quaint street in Holland can be when it snows.

"Darling," I cried, "look at our special Christmas gift, straight from heaven."

Wally struggled to a sitting position, and I held the curtains aside for him. His eyes sparkled a bit between red swollen lids, and his pocked lips broke into a smile.

"Isn't it beautiful?" I whispered.

"Indeed."

We were both silent for a long minute, just wondering at the rare beauty. Then he lay back on his pillow. Reaching out and squeezing my hand, he said, "You know, Dear, I think I feel a little better. How about a cup of bouillon and a hot water bottle? I sure don't want you out there slipping around in all that snow."

Somehow I managed to find a tiny white spot on his forehead and planted a kiss there. Scurrying down the stairs for bouillon, I knew God had answered my plea for forgiveness, healing, and strength.

"My dearest Lord Jesus," I whispered my prayer, "thank you. A white Christmas! You do care a lot."

Then, switching on the kitchen light, I added: "And thanks

so much for making Wally comfortable. You're great, Lord."

That night was the turning point in the chicken pox. I never had to make that trip to the dispensary.

Today I look back and remember it all as the Christmas when God showed me his love in a special way—love that reaches down into life's moments and surprises us with rare treats of beauty.

From *Home Life*, Dec. 1974. © Copyright 1974 The Sunday School Board of the Southern Baptist Convention. All rights reserved. Used by permission.

APPENDIX TWO

GLOSSARY OF WRITER'S TERMS

Anecdote: Short, poignant real-life story, usually used to illustrate one single point.

Argumentation: Form of writing that persuades a reader to consider a change in beliefs, attitudes, or actions.

As-told-to Story: True story I write as a first-person account, but about someone else, e.g., Susan Smith, as told to Mary Jones.

Blue Pencil: To edit a manuscript.

Book Outline: Usually a chapter summary outline, giving a brief overview of the intended contents of a book. Used as part of a book proposal package.

Book Proposal: Package submitted to an editor, including query letter, chapter summary outline, and usually one to three sample chapters.

Bridge: Short passage between the introduction or lead and body of a story or article. Its function is to make the transition between the story parts smooth and easy to follow.

Byline: Author's name appearing with his printed work.

Caption: Title or explanation of a photograph or artwork.

Character Sketch: Biographical personality article.

Clichés: Once-bright, colorful, mood-inducing, active words and phrases that, through overuse, have become tarnished, unimaginative, and meaningless.

Collaboration: Project written by two or more people working together. Also called Co-authoring.

Copy: Unprinted manuscript.

Cover Letter: Letter of explanation accompanying a manuscript. Not needed for most submissions.

Creative Cycle: Normal progression of the creative process from vague creative urge through to completion of a project and ensuing dormant period.

Credits: List of published works of an author.

Description: Form of writing showing how a thing looks, feels, smells, sounds, tastes, or affects the emotions.

Devotional: Short piece or book which shares personal spiritual discovery, inspires to worship, challenges to commitment and/or action, encourages.

Dialogue: Written conversation between story characters.

Editorial Guidelines: Information available from publishers to guide writers in the preparation and submission of materials that meet editorial requirements.

Epigram: Short, pithy statement of truth. Often humorous or paradoxical.

Essay: Short composition on a single subject, usually presenting writer's opinion.

Exposition: Form of writing that explains, defines, interprets, informs, or gives directions.

Feature Article: Full-length piece of nonfiction (1500 – 3000 words) which develops a theme and illustrates it.

Filler: Short piece of material used to fill in small space on a magazine page (e.g., anecdote, quotation, poetry, epigram, joke, puzzle).

First-person Story: True story I write about my own experience.

Flashback: Incident from the past, told out of sequence in a story for the purpose of providing background information or motivation for character action.

Flow: Smooth movement of thoughts and words from line to line, sentence to sentence, paragraph to paragraph.

259

Focus: Narrowing size and complexity of an idea to make it meet specific needs.

Force: Powerful impact made on the reader by written words and their arrangement.

Frame: Introduction and/or conclusion used as a setting for a story or an article.

Free-lance Writer: Writer who is not on a salary for writing, but sells his material usually to a variety of markets.

Fresh Angle: New approach to an old topic.

Galleys: Proof copy of typeset manuscript, usually printed in continuous sheets without page numbers. Used for final corrections by author and editors before printing.

Ghost Writing: Writing someone else's story without using your own byline.

Glossy Photo: Black and white photo developed on glossy paper.

Hook: Opening lines of a piece, designed to reach out and hook the reader. Also called the Lead.

House Organ: Official magazine or newspaper of a business, denomination, or other organization.

How-to: Article or book which explains how to do or make something.

Imagery: Picture language using concrete visual words to communicate abstract concepts.

Inspirational: Articles, stories, or books written for the purpose of uplifting and inspiring readers to positive thoughts and noble, unselfish deeds.

Journal: Regular personal record of reactions to and feelings about life, devotional thoughts, and learned principles. A type of diary of the soul.

Journalism: Writing of stories by telling them in a straight reportorial style, usually for newspapers or newsletters.

Lead: See "Hook."

Media: Means of communicating ideas and facts; e.g., radio, books, movies.

Model Release: Signed permission from the subject of a photograph for a photographer to use a photograph for sale purposes.

Multiple Submission: Submission of more than one manuscript to a single publisher at one time.

Narration: Telling of a story in sequential order.

Narrative: Style of writing which depends on the telling of events in sequence.

On Acceptance: Magazine pays writer when accepting his manuscript.

On Approval: Editor wants to see author's material so he can evaluate it for possible publication.

On Assignment: Writing something at the specific request of an editor.

On Publication: Magazine pays writer when publishing his manuscript.

On Speculation: Editor agrees to look at writer's material without prior commitment to purchase it.

Personal Experience Story: Account of real-life experience.

Persuasion: See "Argumentation."

Photo Essay: Set of photographs that develop or illustrate a theme. Presented either alone or with a short (often poetic) text.

Plant: Idea important to the resolution of a story conflict; hinted at early in the story.

Plot: Story line that progressively develops a theme via conflict, builds to a climax, and ends in a satisfying resolution.

Point of View: Angle from which a story is told; e.g., first person ("I").

Polishing: Rewriting and revising the material.

Profile: See "Character Sketch."

Public Domain: Published material either never copyrighted or with expired copyright.

Query: Letter to editor, soliciting interest in an idea.

Reader Takeaway: Lesson the reader learns from a story.

Reader's Guide to Periodical Literature: Monthly subject, title, and author listing of all articles printed in most magazines. Available in public libraries.

Red String: Strong central theme running through a piece.

Research: Process of gathering materials to collect or verify facts or to enrich background on a subject. Involves book searching, interviewing, travel, planned experiences.

Rights: Legal right to publish or submit for publication written manuscripts or previously printed work:
First Rights: Editor buys the right to print your material for the first time.
Reprint Rights: Editor buys the right to reprint published work.
Second Rights: Editor buys the right to print materials for the second time. Better to offer him reprint rights.
All Rights: Editor buys the sole rights to publish writer's material in whatever form he desires. No editor can purchase these rights without a signed permission from the author. Some editors will reassign rights upon request, after first publication.
Subsidiary Rights: rights to sell book club, movie, translation, and other rights on a book. These rights usually go by contract to the book editor.

Rough Draft: First writing of an article (or other material) before revisions.

Royalties: Amount paid to author by book publisher, based on contracted percentage of retail sales.

262

SASE: Self-addressed, stamped envelope, enclosed with every manuscript, to insure that an editor will return it if he cannot use it.

Self-help: Type of article or book giving information and inspiration to a reader to solve problems or cope with life.

Show-and-tell Writing: Instead of straight narrative, it paints word pictures to engage the reader in the story.

Simultaneous Submission: Submitting identical copies of a manuscript to more than one editor at a time.

Slant: Approach to a subject, tailored to attract and meet needs of the target audience.

Spin-off Ideas: Ideas suggested by a current writing project.

Staff-written Material: Material written by a magazine staff.

Stream-of-consciousness Writing: Writing down all that comes to mind, as it comes, without preconceived plan or conscious direction.

Stringer: News reporter submitting materials to a newspaper on a regular basis, usually from a specific geographical area.

Structure: Plan of one's writing with a beginning, middle, and ending held together cohesively.

Style: The way a person writes; e.g., formal, chatty, stiff.

Subsidy Publisher: Book publisher that prints books at author's expense and does not pay royalties. To be avoided!

Tearsheet: Magazine or newspaper pages with writer's published work, usually to be submitted to another publisher for reprint.

Theme: Idea, viewpoint, subject of a work. Must be clear, significant, and integrated into entire manuscript.

Thesis: Summary of main ideas given in a single sentence.

Tight Writing: Writing that eliminates unnecessary words and phrases and replaces weak words with effective ones.

Transition: Word, phrase, paragraph, or whole scene which forms a bridge between parts of an article or a story.

Transparency: Colored slide photograph.

Twist: Surprise element in the ending or solution of a story or an article.

Universal Appeal: Quality in written material which makes it attractive and helpful to a wide audience of readers.

Unsolicited Manuscripts: Manuscripts not requested or assigned by an editor.

Vanity Publisher: See "Subsidy Publisher."

Viewpoint: Approach or basic opinion of the author; influences how he treats a subject.

Vignette: Brief scene or story which introduces a character.

Writer's Block: Time when the writer seems unable to find ideas or make himself work on the ideas he has.

Zoom Lens Technique: Method of focusing an idea from general to specific, from vague to sharp, broad to narrow, distant to close-up.

HELPS FOR GROUPS AND CLASSES USING THIS BOOK

WRITERS' GROUPS

1. Read the text at home or in sessions.
2. Assign a leader to lead the discussion of text and assignments
   a. One leader to lead every session
   b. Rotate leaders, so a different person takes the responsibility each meeting.

TEACHERS OF CLASSES

Alternatives:
1. Use the text as a basis for class structure.
2. Supplement and adapt the text for class instruction.
3. Prepare your own lessons and use the text for extra reading, with or without assignments.

SOME SUGGESTED CLASS OR GROUP EXERCISES FOR EACH LESSON

Lessons are designed to help students learn gradually to share their work in a group. Assignments are begun at the most unthreatening level possible and lead the shy student step by step to share more and more. If you are going to make this work, consider the following suggestions for group participation:

1. Encourage full participation, but never coerce or go around the circle. Exercises involve lots of personal sharing and may be unduly threatening to shy students, who may have never shown anyone their written work.
2. Never pass judgment on students' opinions. When dealing with anything as creative as written expression, do all you can to preserve the fragile self-image of all.
   CAUTION: Do not give undeserved praise or encourage-

266

ment. Writers' groups are not mutual admiration societies. Find a helpful balance.

3. Some students will never be able to bring themselves to read their own work aloud in a group. Respect this inability and offer to read their work for them.

Lesson One

Part 1: Students share verbally or on paper why and what they want to write, and what writing experience they have had.

Part 2: Students spend 10—15 minutes in class recording all sensory impressions possible from the immediate environment. Include the general mood of the room. You may ask all who are interested to write their impressions in the form of a poem. In discussion, share discoveries.

Lesson Two

Part 1: Students share markets they know about and would like to write for.

Part 2: Give students identical copies of a sample piece of any kind of writing. Have them read through and list examples of good and bad word choices. Share their findings and explain why they were good or bad choices.

Lesson Three

Part 1: Students list the following information about themselves: home background, places they've lived, hobbies and special interests, vacation preferences, ministry activities, strong opinions, books and magazines they read.

Part 2: Give the class the following simple sentence:

The boy walked home.

Allow 15—20 minutes for all to rewrite the sentence to make it lively, colorful, and specific. Then share their results, remembering that there is no single right or wrong way to do it. Call attention to the variety of results.

Lesson Four

Part 1: Students share their favorite books and magazines and tell why they like them and what they have learned about writing, from their reading.

Part 2: Choose several paragraphs from any kind of writing. Give identical copies to students. As a class, analyze each paragraph, looking for (1) number of words, (2) type of paragraph, (3) topic sentence, and (4) evaluation. In other words, *Is the paragraph clear? Forceful? Unified?*

Lesson Five

Part 1: Students make lists of disciplines they need to work on and plan specific ways to do this.

Part 2: Students share writing ideas. Take a sample idea (not one of theirs), and lead class in evaluating it by the nine points on their worksheets.

Lesson Six

Part 1: Students analyze their equipment and work areas and make specific plans for improving both.

Part 2: Do Assignment 3 in class and discuss findings.

Lesson Seven

Part 1: Students share information about markets they are studying.

Part 2: Arrange to meet for this session in your local public library (or school library). Have the librarian give you a tour of the library and point out things of special interest to writers. You may allow time for students to do Assignment 2 while you are there and report back for discussion, at the end of the time. (Investigate the possibility of meeting in a library conference room.)

Lesson Eight

Part 1: Give students identical copies of a personal experience story. Discuss why it was or was not well structured.

Part 2: Have students identify and discuss the following items for the story they evaluated in Part 1:

(1) Theme, (2) Purpose, (3) Market, (4) Form, (5) Outline.

Lesson Nine

Part 1: Lead discussion of special problem areas students face in handling responsibilities covered in the text. Spend some time praying about these needs.

Part 2: Do Assignment 1 in class and discuss it.

Lesson Ten

  Part 1: Read a sample article or story and discuss the style, using the following questions: (1) What kind of style is it? (2) Does it communicate effectively? (3) Is it appropriate to the theme? (4) What does it tell you about the author? (5) Does it attract the target audience?

  Part 2: Read "Then Came Christmas" (on pages 251—255) in class, and discuss its Plan Worksheet and Structural Pattern.

Lesson Eleven

  Part 1: Discuss use of typing format guide and manuscript submission form.

  Part 2: Share a sample unpolished manuscript and rewrite and polish it in group discussion. Simulate a critique group. You may wish to spend your entire next class session critiquing manuscripts that students will polish after this lesson. If so, take time in class to review the guidelines for critique groups (Appendix 5).

Lesson Twelve

  Encourage students to share what they feel they have gained from this course, how their goals have changed since Lesson 1, what they feel about their writing calling, and what specific steps they plan to take next.

Further Sessions:

  Use additional exercises in Appendix 4 for future class sessions or group meetings.

APPENDIX FOUR

ADDITIONAL WRITING ASSIGNMENTS

FOUR BASIC FORMS OF WRITING
Narration: Tells a story.
Exposition: Explains ideas.
Description: Paints word pictures and sets moods.
Argumentation: Persuades the reader.

NARRATION: This is the form studied in this book.

EXPOSITION
1. Functions: to explain, inform, interpret, define, give directions
2. Goal: clarity
3. Appeal: to the intellect
4. Forms of exposition:
    a. Definitions
    b. Directions (how-to, recipes, processes)
    c. Mechanisms and Organizations (how things work, how things are organized, how something happened)
    d. Analysis (takes a subject apart, examines component parts and relationships)
    e. Essays (expositions of personal opinion)
5. Components of expositional writing:
    a. Organization of thought
    b. Specific detail
    c. Examples
    d. Contrast and comparison
    e. Division (explains parts)
    f. Origin
Assignment:
Write an essay on one of the fruits of the Spirit.

DESCRIPTION
1. Functions:
    a. Leads into other things

270

b. Sets scenes
c. Draws the reader into the picture by
   Employing all the senses
   Involving the emotions
   Orienting the reader
2. Goal: provides color and interest
3. Appeal: to the senses and the emotions
4. Components:
   a. Color
   b. Shape
   c. Size
   d. Movement
   e. Mood
5. How to write a good description:
   a. Perceive clearly and accurately.
   b. Choose correct words.
   c. Arrange details well.
   d. Choose details that fit the theme.
6. Common pitfalls of descriptive writing:
   a. Too many similes
   b. Dullness
   c. Lengthiness and wordiness
   d. Improper placement (e.g., do not place long descriptions in action spots)
   e. Lack of objectivity or perspective

Assignment:

Write a clear, clean description of one of the following:
   Something from your past
   A familiar place
   A new place
   Your best friend
   A scene of action with description interspersed.

ARGUMENTATION (Also called PERSUASION)
1. Functions:
   a. Stimulates disinterested persons to think and act
   b. Changes the minds and actions of persons hostile to your ideas

    c. Confirms ideas of those who agree with you and increases their confidence and/or commitment to truth

2. Appeal: to the intellect and the emotions
3. Characteristics of good argumentation:
   a. Logically sound and intellectually honest
   b. Based on reason, with emotions used only to reinforce that reason
   c. Provides clarifying information and illuminates all sides of an issue
   d. Projects author-image of
      Sincerity
      Genuine commitment to a cause
      Responsibility
      Honorable intentions
      Fairness
4. Forms of argumentation:
   a. Essays
   b. Editorials
   c. Tracts
   d. P. R. and advertising
5. How to write argumentation:
   a. Collect complete facts and ideas.
   b. Write your thesis and examine it to be sure you can live with and support it.
   c. Examine all the important issues involved; define each issue clearly.
   d. Support thesis with adequate evidence.
   e. Organize logically.
   f. Draw a pointed conclusion.
6. Pitfalls to avoid in argumentation writing:
   a. Improper use of analogy (comparison and contrast)
   b. Argument against a man rather than against his cause
   c. Appealing only to emotions without a logical base
   d. Authoritarianism, bigotry, and name-calling
   e. Evading the real issue by getting sidetracked on minor issues
   d. Oversimplification

Assignment:
Write either an opinion essay or a tract.

INTERVIEWING TIPS

WHY INTERVIEW?
1. Basic research form for all people-centered articles
2. Firsthand sources are always best
3. Establishes new friendships and contacts for future writing projects

KINDS OF INTERVIEWS
1. Press conference
2. Personal, face-to-face interview
3. Telephone interview
4. Mail interview

PREPARING FOR AN INTERVIEW
1. Research your subject. Learn all you can about the person and your topic before the interview.
2. Make either no outline or a tentative outline before the interview.
3. Make an appointment that suits your subject.
4. Make a tentative list of questions to ask:
   a. Opinion-evoking questions that cannot be answered with "yes" or "no"
   b. Specific questions
5. Prepare yourself—be neat, enthusiastic, courteous.
6. Pray for a calm, sensitive spirit and an alert mind.
7. Prepare to tape or take notes.
8. Approach your subject with confidence and businesslike attitudes.

CONDUCTING THE INTERVIEW
1. Put your subject at ease by:
   a. Pronouncing his name correctly.
   b. Complimenting him on something
   c. Being open, not argumentative
   d. Relaxing
   e. Starting with small talk and letting him choose the direction of the opening get-acquainted minutes.

2. Begin with simple, noncontroversial questions.
3. Solicit the following information:
   a. Things unobtainable elsewhere
   b. Unique things about your subject—mannerisms, opinions, achievements, personality, physical features
   c. Sparkling anecdotes
   d. Lead angles
   e. Possibilities for other stories
   f. Always ask him, "Why?"
   g. Keep alert to anything your reader would like to know or needs to know.
4. Keep the interview moving. Don't get sidetracked, but be sensitive to special new angles that need to be pursued.
5. Verify statements as you go. Ask him to repeat if you are unsure.
6. Be a good listener. You are not being interviewed.
7. Mentally edit your outline as you listen. But not at the expense of appearing distracted!
8. Agree to check direct quotes or matters of fact later, before you submit your manuscript.

ENDING THE INTERVIEW
1. Stop on time as previously agreed, unless the interviewee wishes to continue.
2. Go back and verify facts or quotes that are vital.
3. Tell him you will call if you have further questions.
4. Do not promise to let him see the completed article before it is printed.
5. After you close your notebook, keep your ears open and mind alert. The best things usually come when the subject feels the interview is over—especially at the door.

AFTER THE INTERVIEW
1. Transcribe all notes, filling in gaps, on the typewriter, *immediately*.
2. Send a thank-you note to your subject. Say something complimentary about the interview.
3. Call the subject to check on details, if necessary.

4. Respect confidences your subject shared with you.
5. Notify your subject when you know the date of publication.
6. Send him an autographed copy of the article.
7. Keep his name, address, and a record of the interview.
8. Keep in touch with your subject.

ASSIGNMENT:
Plan and conduct an interview.

THE PERSONALITY PROFILE

WHAT IS IT?
A biographical article presenting a single aspect of some person's life and character.

SOURCES OF PERSONALITY PROFILE SUBJECTS
1. Personal acquaintances
2. Historical research
3. Organizations and their leaders
4. The media (radio, newspapers, TV, magazines, etc.)

USABLE TYPES OF PERSONALITY PROFILES
1. Overcoming handicaps and solving problems
2. Special ministries, hobbies, occupations
3. Conversion experiences
4. Vignettes (brief story glimpses into character)
5. Unusual experiences
6. Interesting facts about well-known people

STRUCTURE OF PERSONALITY PROFILES
1. Personal experience, fictional plot plan structure
2. Article structure

HOW TO WRITE THE PERSONALITY PROFILE

1. Slant it for the specific market you are aiming for.
2. Narrow the focus to a single:
   a. Achievement
   b. Experience
   c. Philosophy or characteristic.
3. Research thoroughly:
   a. Background reading
   b. Interviewing the subject
   c. Interviewing friends, family, associates of subject.
4. Show; do not just tell.
5. Write either in the first person "as-told-to" or the third person.
6. Make effective use of anecdotes, quotes, observations. Keep the human interest factor at the top of your list.
7. Structure it well and write as well as you can.

ASSIGNMENT:

1. Find at least three personality profile articles in magazines and read them. Did their authors follow the guidelines given in the above list?
2. Choose a subject and write your own personality profile.

THE DEVOTIONAL

WHAT IS IT?

A short nonfiction piece (100–300 words) which:

1. Shares a personal discovery of truth
2. Stresses spiritual principles
3. Reminds the reader of the greatness of God and inspires to worship and awe
4. Challenges the reader, inspiring him to deepen or renew his commitment to Jesus Christ OR
   Gives the reader new hope or guidance in handling the challenges of life.

WHAT FORMS DO DEVOTIONALS TAKE?

1. A prayer
2. Paraphrased psalm or other Scripture passage
3. Anecdote with a summary
4. Personal experience, with or without commentary frame
5. Biblical exposition
6. Inspirational meditation on a Scripture verse
7. Anecdote and exposition
8. Others—parable, mood piece, poem, etc.

HOW TO WRITE A DEVOTIONAL

1. Pick one finely focused theme.
2. Pick a form (you may need to experiment with several).
3. Use Scripture carefully
   a. Quote it correctly
   b. Quote it briefly
   c. Include references
   d. Make sure it proves your point.
4. Write well by
   a. Not preaching
   b. Not overusing the word *I*
   c. Explaining backgrounds briefly (e.g., identify people, places, movements; define words)
   d. Using a warm, personal, positive, colorful style
   e. Structuring it well
   f. Keeping it short.

ASSIGNMENT:
Write a devotional.

THE CHURCH NEWS STORY

TWO TYPES OF NEWS STORIES

1. News feature—built on an article structure
2. Straight news story

a. Basic facts in the first paragraph
b. Facts of lesser importance in the following paragraphs
It is read, written, edited, and printed in a hurry. Cutting is done from the bottom up, so details of decreasing interest and importance belong on the bottom.

FUNCTIONS OF CHURCH NEWS RELEASES
1. Public awareness of church in the community
   Caution: Make the image a good one!
2. Public information about the church
3. Public exposure of a message
4. Public involvement in the church program

WHAT MAKES A GOOD CHURCH NEWS ITEM?
1. Event with some historical community significance
2. Event with social or cultural community significance
3. Message delivered by some visiting celebrity
4. Message dealing with current community issue
5. Unusual programs that meet needs
6. Stories of positive action taken by church members

ASSIGNMENT:
1. Read local church news items and evaluate their worth.
2. Pick some item of church news you feel is significant; plan and write it.

THE HOW-TO ARTICLE
WHAT IS IT?
Short piece of nonfiction that offers the reader advice and/or instructions for doing something that will improve his life and/or ministry.

HOW TO WRITE A HOW-TO ARTICLE
1. Make a list of ideas of things you have learned to do, or that people you know have learned to do.

2. Choose an idea of significance with some unique feature.
3. Narrow the focus of your article to be practical.
4. Plan your article
   a. Opening to attract someone to want to do it
   b. Theme sentence: Promise what you are going to show the reader.
   c. Directions:
      Lists of materials in detail. Where to find them, if unusual. May include approximate costs. Step-by-step instructions. Photos and diagrams may be helpful.
      Warn of pitfalls and don'ts.
   d. Challenge:
      Final pithy clincher to assure and inspire the reader.
5. Keep it between one or two paragraphs and 1500 words.
6. I-you point of view is best. Avoid a superior attitude; show you are learning and sharing this learning.
7. Write in a brief, simple, helpful, unornamented style. Numbered lists increase readability and applicability.
8. Make the title:
   a. Catchy
   b. Authentic—promise what you plan to deliver
   c. Keyed to readership
      (Does not always have to include words "how to").
9. Ask a person who knows nothing about the subject to read your piece and make sure he or she understands it well and can do what you have advised.

ASSIGNMENT:
1. Read several how-to articles and evaluate them.
2. Write a how-to article.

THE FILLER
WHAT IS IT?
A short item of a line or two up to 1,000 words, that generally does one of three things:

1. Fills up extra space in a magazine.
2. Appears as a regular featured column.
3. Does something special.

KINDS OF FILLERS

1. *Epigram:* Short pithy statement, expressing some witty idea in memorable fashion.
2. *Bright Saying:* Clever saying, usually from a child. A glimpse of the world seen through a twinkling eye.
3. *Anecdote:* Story in miniature.
4. *Quotations:* From famous or unknown people
   a. Some written singly as one-liners that pack a punch.
   b. Groups of quotations around a single theme are called "round-up articles."
5. *Fact Fillers:* Short, objective presentation of interesting facts of all kinds (20 – 300 words).
6. *Hint and Advice:* Household hints, crafts ideas, Christian Ed suggestions. . . .
7. *Devotional:* Short piece of a devotional nature.
8. *Paraphrase or Adaptation:* Rewriting a familiar passage of Scripture in your own words and with a new slant.
9. *Prayer:* Theme expressed in the form of personal or collective prayer.
10. *Light Verse:* Light and usually humorous in content. Relies on puns, rhyme, catchy phrases, twists of clichés, literal interpretations of imagery phrases.
11. *Quizzes and Puzzles:* Mostly for children's magazines.
12. *Book Review:* Short analysis of a book and its merits, designed to help the reader decide whether to purchase a book.
13. *Newspaper or Magazine Column:* Regular feature in a periodical. May be local or syndicated. May be on a given theme or a variety of themes.
14. *Letter to the Editor:* Make it a sane, logical demonstration of Christian restraint and responsibility.
15. *Essay:* Opinion piece designed to help change the reader's mind.
16. *List:* Practical list of things to do or to try or to check out. Geared to the specific needs of the reader.

17. *Interview:* Short interview with one person about a single topic of interest to readers.
18. *Character Vignette:* Single incident picture that highlights some person's commendable character trait.
19. *Short How-to:* Under 1,000-word treatment of how to do something specific.

ASSIGNMENT:
1. Make a collection of different kinds of fillers, and study them for style and idea types.
2. Write one or more fillers.

THE TRACT
WHAT IS IT?
A short leaflet, presenting the plan of salvation or some specific challenge for Christian living. Designed usually as an evangelistic tool.

KINDS OF TRACTS
1. Seasonal
2. Informational
3. Testimonial
4. Shock treatment
5. Interest-oriented
6. Need-oriented
7. Analogies

SPECIAL GUIDELINES FOR WRITING TRACTS
1. Write an attractive lead.
2. Do not use "Christianese" language.
3. Do not preach.
4. Be brief.
5. Use Scripture references when quoting Scripture.

6. Work for grabbing and authentic short titles.
7. Do not try to accomplish too much.
8. Use language and style appropriate to the message and target audience.

ASSIGNMENT:
1. Collect and evaluate tracts.
2. Write a tract.

APPENDIX FIVE

CHECKLISTS FOR CRITIQUING SPECIAL FORMS

THE QUERY LETTER

1. Have I kept it short? (one or two pages of single-spaced typing, maximum)
2. Have I made it attractive? Is this a sample of my best writing?
3. Have I included pertinent details an editor needs in order to make a decision about:
   a. My idea?
   b. My authority to write about this subject?
   c. My excitement about writing about this subject?
   d. My thesis?
   e. My ability to handle the subject?
   f. Intended word length?
4. Is the letter well organized?
5. If I include an outline, is it well thought out, well structured? Does it give an accurate picture of the article I propose?
6. Have I shown a concern for the editor and his needs? Or simply my own enthusiasm and need for expression?
7. Have I been courteous to the editor, refraining from threats (implied or stated), unreasonable demands, and assurances that "God gave me this manuscript verbatim and told me to send it to you"?
8. Have I asked for editorial guidelines for this piece?
9. Am I familiar with the magazine I am querying? Does my letter reveal such familiarity?
10. Did I address the editor by name?
11. Have I submitted only one idea per query?

THE PERSONAL EXPERIENCE

1. What is unique about this experience? What is my slant on it?

2. Have I hit on the proper combination of brevity and clarity?
3. Have I been true to the facts?
4. Have I admitted my own weaknesses and my need for growth?
5. What is the value of this story to my projected readers?
6. Have I preached a sermon or shared an experience in learning and growth?
7. How believable are my characters?
8. Will anyone be damaged or offended by this story's publication?
9. Have I included the three essential elements of a personal experience story—problem, solution, and outcome?

THE PERSONALITY PROFILE

1. What is unique about this person? A handicap? An achievement? A dramatic experience? A conversion? A philosophy?
2. Can this story help my target readers?
3. Did I acquire adequate background information to handle it well?
4. Is the story simply sensational? Or does it paint a vivid picture of God at work in a human life? Does it glorify a person? Or God?
5. Have I presented a proper balance between the *before* (sin) and *after* (deliverance) so that my readers will remember my point longer than the scandalous features of the story?
6. Will publication of this vignette harm the person I have written about? Will it harm his family? His friends? The church?

THE DEVOTIONAL

1. Have I picked a single poignant theme?
2. Does the form I have chosen communicate my message most effectively (forms include prayer, paraphrased psalm, or other Scripture; personal experience story, either with or without a frame; inspirational meditation; parable; mood piece; poetic prose; letter)?

3. Have I been brief and to the point?
4. Have I avoided a preachy tone? Did I share myself?
5. Did I overuse the word *I?*
6. Did I strain an analogy to make a point?
7. Did I use a warm, personal, fresh, and informal style?
8. Did I structure it well? Is there a clearly defined beginning, middle, and ending?
9. Did I appeal to my readers' heart? To their intellect? To their will?
10. Did I make God exceedingly attractive?
11. Did I control my quotation of Scripture, limiting it to one or two brief quotes?
12. What did I offer my reader?
13. Does this devotional represent my best writing skills, polished and honed to be worthy of God's name?

THE CHURCH NEWS STORY

1. Is this a fact story that gives information? Or is it a quote story that gives opinions?
2. What is the function of this news story? Public awareness of our church? Public information about our church? Public exposure to a message? Limited audience information? (denominational magazines)
3. Have I included all the essential facts in the first oneto three-sentence paragraph?
4. Are my subject and technique truly appealing to my audience?
5. Does this story represent my best writing?
6. Have I avoided churchy language? Pushiness? Preachiness?

THE HOW-TO ARTICLE

1. Is it short and to the point?
2. Is it tightly written? Are there things (words, paragraphs, whole ideas) I could cut out and still say what I want to say?
3. Is it clear? (Ask someone unfamiliar with your topic or procedure to read it and tell you what it says to him.)

4. Is it written in an interesting way? (Dullness never inspires action.)
5. Is it helpful? Specific?
6. Does it offer a new subject? Or a new angle on an old subject?
7. Is it significant? How many people will care to read it?
8. Do you have an arresting lead?
9. Did you state your theme in a single sentence near the beginning?
10. Have you listed *all* materials needed (down to the last nail or toothpick)?
11. Are your directions given in logical, procedural, step-by-step order?
12. Are there pitfalls, special difficulties, and/or hazzards involved in this project? If so, have you warned your reader about them and told him how to avoid them?
13. Have you ended on a challenging note that will reach out and grab your reader?
14. Is the title catchy? Does it accurately represent the intent of your article? Is it appropriate and/or appealing to your intended readership?

THE TRACT
1. What was my purpose for writing this tract? What was my target audience? What was my expected response?
2. Is it realistic to expect to accomplish all this in 500 words or less?
3. Have I avoided offensive language (technical theological terminology and Christianese)? Preachy attitudes? Obnoxious approach?
4. Do I have an effective title?
5. Have I included references with all the Scriptures I have quoted?
6. Have I avoided strained analogies and hokey stories?
7. What have I offered the reader?
8. Have I avoided dullness? Stuffiness? Naiveté?
9. Will my tract truly attract people to God? Or will it give them reason to call him shoddy?

APPENDIX SIX

EVALUATING A BOOK IDEA

"You mean you have had a book published?" How often I am addressed in this way by some overawed stranger who has just learned of my profession. The words always weigh heavy with wonder and incredulity. Our society has the idea that to write a book is to "arrive," to become an unusual human specimen. The reaction is not far removed from worship.

To write a book can be a prestigious thing. But if it is, that is because it demands such a tremendous amount of disciplined thinking, heart-searching, and dedication to duty. When done rightly, book writing results from excruciating work. Further, it involves a special kind of process, quite different from the production of a shorter work. It demands a unique level of stick-to-itiveness to live with the same project for months, even years without tiring of it or losing powers of intense struggle with it.

A book project is not recommended as a starting point for beginners. Yet, because so many would-be writers approach the writing discipline with a book idea in mind, I want to give you some suggestions and checklists to enable you to determine whether indeed you are ready to think about writing that book that seems to be calling you. In order to sort out the romance from the reality of your dreams and fit them into a practical time frame, you need to answer three basic questions:

1. Is my idea a book or an article?
2. Should I write this book? If so, am I ready to begin?
3. How shall I prepare to write this book?

BOOK IDEAS VERSUS ARTICLE IDEAS

Does my idea warrant development as a book or would it be better as an article?

A book *is not:*

1. An article on a simple subject, padded with enough anecdotes, descriptions, philosophizings, quotations, and the like to fill 100 or more pages between two covers.
2. A loose collection of vaguely related articles, vignettes, poems, sermons, or other short works.
3. A detailed autobiography or lengthy family history that fascinates the writer and therefore is as sure to sell as popcorn at a football game.

A book *is:*

1. A work of 10,000 to 100,000 words or more.
2. A work with complexity of idea and strength of theme adequate to sustain a reader's interest for the extended period of time it takes to dig through all those thousands of words.

    It may be an anthology, or collection of articles, poems, stories, even sermons. However, these need to be so tightly unified in theme and form that the reader is unaware that they are collections. He thinks of them, rather, as a complete book unit.
3. A work that usually demands a great deal more research than an article. You need many more quotes, statistics, illustrations, opinions, and bits of local color for a book than for an article. All of these are necessary, however, not for padding, but as a part of developing significant themes.
4. A work with sufficient interest intensity to arrest the reader all on its own and convince him it is worth the price he will pay for a single-subject volume. A magazine article will go home with the reader who buys that magazine out of loyalty to the magazine (often by subscription), for the pictures, or for some other articles or feature materials. A book has to draw the reader on its own merit and deliver what the cover promises.

To distinguish an *article* from a *book* idea, ask yourself: *Is my idea sufficiently complex, practical, colorful, and intensely interesting to entice thousands of readers to part with their money in order to buy it and then to give it the hours required to carry them through its several thousands of words and be glad they read it?*

TO WRITE OR NOT TO WRITE A BOOK

Should you attempt to write this book? If so, are you ready to begin?

The chances are that provided your idea is truly significant, timely, and needed, if you do not write the book, someone else will. In fact, the idea has probably occurred to some editor, and he may be looking for the right person to write it. The questions at issue, then, are these:

Should it be written?

If so, am I the person to do it?

Your prospective editor will ask these questions when he reads your book proposal. So prepare to defend your "yes" answers to both questions before you approach him. To determine these answers, go through the following checklist and be completely honest with each question. Until you have answered them, you are not ready to consider writing a book.

SELF-APPRAISAL CHECKLIST

Basic Considerations: Do I know what I am trying to do?
1. Why do I want to write this book? To acquire fame or fortune? To spout off anger or expose some evil? To minister to the needs of the Body of Christ? To fulfill my dreams? To prove myself to someone?
2. Who is my target audience? Age group? Occupational group? Sex? Interest group? (Visualize your reader sitting across the room from you as you write.)
3. What do I want to say? Can I summarize my theme in a twenty-five to fifty-word paragraph? (If not, your idea is not clear enough to work on or even test for validity.)
4. What response do I expect from my readers? Mental or spiritual stimulation? Change of mind or attitudes? Worship? Action? (Be specific.)

Responsibility: Do I dare to write this book?
5. Am I convinced enough of my ideas that I dare to put them out into nationwide (or worldwide) circulation

where they will affect thousands of lives? (If not, wait until you have wrestled with them long enough to be sure.)

6. Does my priority-and-duty system allow me to expend the time and energy required to finish this book?

7. Will anyone be hurt by this book if I write it? (family, friends, organization, Body of Christ, name of Christ)

Validity: Is my idea valid and worth a complete book?

8. Do I strongly believe in it myself? Will I still believe in it ten years from now?

9. Does it carry intense interest value for my target audience? For how wide an audience? (A publisher must sell at least 5,000 copies to break even on his investment.)

10. Is it helpful? To the people I want to reach? To how many people?

11. What new angle or original viewpoint do I offer? How is my approach different from similar books on the same subject? (Your approach must set it apart from the other books close to it.)

12. How urgent and current is the theme? Can I write it and get it out in time to meet the needs I am aiming for? Is it so tied to contemporary issues that it will be outdated in a year or two? If so, is the need for it sufficiently urgent to warrant the sacrifices demanded in order to produce it in time, under pressure?

13. Does it offer hope to my readers? Can I be positive in my message? Do I have problem solutions to share or am I interested only in exposing difficulties and leaving the reader numb with shock and despair?

14. Is it a sensational story? Does it glorify man and/or describe sin so graphically that God's grace is not the predominant picture planted in the reader's mind? Is God clearly at the center of focus of this book idea?

15. Is there enough material available and does this idea offer sufficient depth and interest content to make it worth a whole book? Or would I do better to confine it to one or more articles?

Qualifications: Am I the right person to write this book?

16. Have I had sufficient experience or training in the subject area to qualify me as an expert?
17. Do my credentials give me an adequate authority image to enable the editor to sell my book?
18. Do I know how to do the research which this project will demand? Is such a process practical for me at this time?
19. Am I genuinely excited about this project? Enough so that I can live and work with it for the next year or two without growing tired of it?
20. Am I willing to research the market thoroughly in order to find the best outlet for my book?
21. Do I have the patience to wait until my research is complete before I start writing? To set the project aside for a time, if need be, until I know the Lord wants me to push ahead with it? To accept long delays in the editorial and publication process as a part of God's perfect timing?
22. Can I take criticism and suggestions from editors? Am I adaptable and willing to work with editors on business details?
23. Am I prepared to take the time and effort to reply and pray for all who will respond to this book with pleas for attention, fellowship, clarification, and help of various sorts?

Someone has said that any Christian book that will bless people's lives must first cost the writer a great deal in personal learning and growth as well as hard work. *Am I willing to make whatever sacrifices this project may involve, for the glory of God through my work?*

PREPARING TO WRITE A BOOK

1. Learn to write and market your materials. Start with the small things—articles, poems, stories, fillers. Master the disciplines of scheduling, planning, polishing, marketing, and editorial relationships. This is the process of becoming

a writer. Do not launch into the book field prematurely, but plan on a long internship, remembering that God has as much time as it takes to get you ready to do his work in his way.

2. Become familiar with the categories of books on the Christian market. They can be broken down as follows:
   a. *Personal experience books:* Stories of what happened to the author; how-to and self-help books about things the author has learned to do or problems he has learned to solve or cope with.
   b. *Personal expression books:* Devotional books, opinion books.
   c. *Research books:* Historical background, Bible studies, commentaries, resource books, histories of the Church, missions, denominations, historical biographies.
   d. *Other people's books:* Biographies, modern histories of families, organizations, missionary ventures, anthologies of essays or articles on a theme, modern translations of old classics, personal stories of other people done in one of several ways:
      1) Straight third-person narrative, with author's byline.
      2) First person as-told-to; e.g., Susan Smith as told to Mary Jones.
      3) First person, with author; e.g., Susan Smith with Mary Jones.
      4) Ghost-written books in which the author writes someone else's story, and only the subject's name appears in the byline. The author's name is not mentioned, even though he does receive a percentage of the royalties. Many authors and editors (myself included) find this practice unethical, as it gives the false impression that the person whose story it is, is also a writer.
   e. *Co-authoring or collaboration:* Books written by two or more people, with equal bylines; e.g., Susan Smith and Mary Jones.
   CAUTION: Other people's stories and collaborations are the most dangerous types of books to write. *Definitely not recommended for beginners.* The number of sticky problems (both financial and social) that can emerge from such

arrangements defies the most fertile imagination. Before you even consider these types of books, get yourself firmly established as a writer and chalk up a lot of practical experience with editors and the business end of writing.

3. Decide which category your idea fits. Then read samples of those types of books. Study them for structure, technique, significance, style, and use of language. Ask the following questions of each book you read at this stage of research:

   a. Did I enjoy it? Why or why not?

   b. What was the number-one outstanding impression it made on me? What is the theme? How significant is it? Did the author stick to it or ramble off on a dozen tangents?

   c. What was the author's tone? Impassioned orator on a soapbox? Prophet with a broken heart? Psalmist at worship? Teacher come alongside to guide the reader? Dull lecturer? Entertaining storyteller?

   d. What makes this book unique from others on the same topic? What authority does the author have to write it? Does he represent himself as having all the answers? Or as a learning, growing person still struggling with important issues?

   e. What makes this book effective? Or ineffective? Would I recommend it to my target audience of readers? Why or why not? What are its strengths? Its weaknesses?

   f. What problems of technique does this author have that I can expect to face in my writing? How does he handle them?

   g. Is the writing quality commendable or deplorable? Are the characters real people? Are they sufficiently motivated in all their actions? Do they grow? Can I identify with them? Learn from them?

   h. Are the ideas in this book arranged in the best order to build toward a climax of thought?

   i. Is this book scripturally sound? Does it honor God?

   j. Which of the following words best describe the book? positive, negative, helpful, trivial, challenging, dull, colorful, stuffy, preachy, wordy, redundant, frivolous, meaty, accurate, sloppy, repulsive, cliché-ridden, trite, stimulating, reverent, fascinating, fresh, relevant, memorable

4. Get acquainted with the book publication process. It is similar to the Idea To Publication process for an article (See page 31). Briefly, it consists of these steps:
   a. Idea and formulation of a theme
   b. Preliminary research
   c. Preparation of tentative outline
   d. Submission of book proposal, which includes:
      1) Query letter
      2) Tentative paragraph outline (one-paragraph summary of each chapter)
      3) Two or three sample chapters (first chapter and one or two others, not necessarily in sequence)
   e. Go-ahead from editor, usually "on approval," meaning he wants to see the whole manuscript before he makes a commitment. Will include editorial suggestions and deadlines, and may be accompanied by a contract.
   f. Further research, preparation, and submission of finished manuscript.
   g. Final acceptance and contract (if not included with *e* above). Usually accompanied by an author information form to be filled out by the author and used by editorial publicity departments in planning the promotion of your book.
   h. Editing of the manuscript:
      1) By editor
      2) By author, as requested by editor
      3) Galley proofs prepared by editor and checked by both editor and author.
   i. Book publication. Happy day when you hold your bound volume in reverent hands, read the pages, and ask, "Did I really write this?"

CAUTION: When choosing a book publisher, take care to avoid any company that charges you a fee for publication and pays no royalties. These are called *vanity* or *subsidy* publishers. After you pay for the publication, you must usually buy the books from them, and you are always left with the advertising and marketing. Many are the woeful stories of eager authors who went this route and are now burdened with several thousand copies of their brainchild stashed away in a garage.

Vanity publishers publish books with little care for quality.

If your book meets the criteria for book publication and is marketable, it will eventually find a *bona fide* publisher to contract for it. If your manuscript is rejected by all the editors on your target list, rethink the idea, upgrade the quality, and talk to God about timing. It may be the wrong time for your message. Or you may need to do some more growing before you are fully ready to consider publication.

Occasionally you will have an idea that is so specialized that no publisher could afford to risk it, but it warrants publication anyway. Perhaps you have ample contacts to market it to the limited audience that needs it. Then self-publication may be justified. But be aware that this involves a great deal of work with layout, typesetting, marketing, and a million and one things you never dreamed of. And *never* in any case resort to a vanity or subsidy publisher.

Ask God to guide you through the responses of editors. Take these verses as your motto:

> Dear brothers, is your life full of difficulties [and rejections]? Then be happy, for when the way is rough, your patience has a chance to grow. So let it grow, and don't try to squirm out of your problems. For when your patience is finally in full bloom, then you [and your manuscript] will be ready for anything, strong in character, full and complete. (James 1:2–4, TLB) (author's insertions in brackets)

5. Study the special techniques of book writing. For this purpose, I recommend the following sources:
   a. Books such as *Writing and Selling the Non-Fiction Book* by Max Gunther
   b. Workshops in local colleges
   c. Writers' conferences
   d. Critique groups of book writers.

Do you still feel compelled to write that book? Reading through all these checklist questions reminds me again that book authoring is indeed an awesome challenge—one I would not dare to tackle without a clear sense of divine mission.

If you were sitting in my office asking my counsel (Don't I see you seated there across the desk from me now?), I would urge you not to stretch and strain to find excuses why you should write a book. Rather, do all you can to get out of it, but be sure to stay wide open to the perfect will and timing of God. That way, when the book begins to gestate and you are tempted to abort the effort, you can always count on the God who pushed you into it to bring you through the birth pangs into the indescribable joy of authorhood.

APPENDIX SEVEN

A WRITER'S FILES

Every serious writer needs some files to keep his working tools organized for handy recall. Here are five files I consider essential:

1. IDEA FILE (or notebook) (For outline, see Lesson 1, pages 31–32)
2. MARKET FILE
   a. Organized by
      type of magazine (Christian ed, women's, juvenile, etc.)
      alphabetical arrangement of magazines
   b. Includes
      sample copies
      editorial guidelines
      market evaluation sheets.
3. SUBJECT FILE
   a. Alphabetical file, with separate folders for each subject (Alcohol, Missions, Families, etc.)
   b. Includes clippings, pamphlets, facts, ideas, observations, quotations, bibliographies, pictures, source addresses)
   c. May also have a folder for sermon notes, another for poetry, another for personal experience stories, another for fiction stories, etc.
4. PROJECT FILE
   a. One folder for each project you are working on or are considering working on. Arrange alphabetically by the working title.
   b. Each folder contains:
      Notes
      Bibliography
      Correspondence concerning the project
      Carbon copy of the submitted manuscript
      All drafts of a manuscript
      Submission records
      Rejection slips.
5. CARD FILE
   You will use this file for at least three different kinds of entries:

a. Market addresses, with record of submissions (See sample in Lesson 11, page 000)
b. Bibliography notes (record of sources of research information)

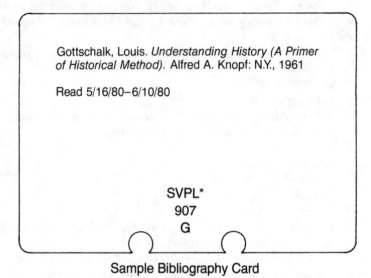

> Gottschalk, Louis. *Understanding History (A Primer of Historical Method)*. Alfred A. Knopf: N.Y., 1961
>
> Read 5/16/80–6/10/80
>
>
>
>   SVPL*
>   907
>   G

Sample Bibliography Card

*Sunnyvale Public Library. If you own the book, record the word *Own*, in this space.

Sometimes I also include notes about the content of the book on this card, particularly if I have not yet read it and want to go back and check it out later.

c. Names and addresses of people and organizations you deal with in your writing. Include dates of correspondence and any other notations of importance for quick reference; e.g., "Send news release on book publication" or "Hobby is collecting antique books" or "Knows president of N. Y. Historical Society."

You may color code the different kinds of entries by using colored cards or by drawing a colored line across the top of the cards. I use a blue line for books, a red line for editorial offices, and a green line for people and organizations.

APPENDIX EIGHT

ORGANIZING A CRITIQUE GROUP

KINDS OF CRITIQUE GROUPS
1. *Christian Writers' Club:* Loosely knit organization of Christians interested in writing. Includes inspirational sharing of market ideas, trends, speakers, and manuscript critiquing. Usually meets at the same time and place on a regular basis. Usually draws some nonwriters who wish they were writers, but rarely write. Majors on fellowship and inspiration.
2. *Critique Workshop:* Small group of committed Christian writers seriously interested in critical assistance for their never-ending flow of projects. May have a constant meeting place or may rotate in the homes of members. Restrict membership to five or six, by invitation only. Emphasis on working.
3. *Correspondence Group:* Round robin of serious publishing writers who submit manuscripts to each other by mail at regular intervals.

RECRUITING MEMBERS FOR THE CRITIQUE GROUP
1. Decide which kind of group you are interested in forming.
2. Some suggested methods for finding members:
   a. Talk to people at writers' conferences and workshops.
   b. Advertise in local churches.
   c. Advertise in newspapers and on the radio.
   d. Place announcements on local college bulletin boards.
   e. Organize round robin or small workshop groups, taking in members on a limited basis and by personal invitation only.
   f. Form a nucleus of regularly publishing writers.

GUIDELINES FOR CONDUCTING THE CRITIQUE GROUP
1. Remember that you are not a mutual admiration society, but a body of Christian artists meeting to encourage and

assist one another in the development of your craft.

2. At the beginning of each session, give each member an opportunity to share his latest accomplishments. Time these reports. *Keep them short!*

3. Occasionally invite speakers. Plan other service activities for the Christian community in your area; e.g., one-day seminars, book fairs, speeches by noted authors.

4. Make sure every member reads and refers often to the booklet *Practical Criticism: Giving It and Taking It* by John Alexander (InterVarsity Press).

5. Review and follow the following guidelines for giving critiques in your sessions:

   a. Let the writer read his manuscript aloud, without interruption. Since poetry should be seen as well as heard, ask the writer to furnish copies so that others can follow along as he reads.

   b. While a manuscript is being read, members should all listen courteously and jot down comments.

   c. Plan for time for every writer to share, if possible. If the group is large, you may rotate so that not everyone reads at every meeting, but everyone gets a turn. Or you may break into smaller groups for the critiquing.

   d. The leader should encourage shy members to participate, but never coerce them to read.

   e. After the manuscript is read, listeners should begin by making positive comments.

   f. Give both general and specific reader comments.

   g. Give concrete suggestions for improvement.

   h. Do not allow one person to monopolize the discussion.

   i. Balance honesty with love in critiquing a work.

   j. Be sensitive to the feelings of writers and offer criticism with caution, according to what you feel a writer is ready to receive. Do not expect the same level of excellence from both beginners and experienced writers.

   k. Never attack the writer's abilities or his person. Merely suggest ideas for improvement.

6. Include sharing of markets, books, technical helps, and other shop talk.

7. Strive and pray for a unified spirit in your group. Your goal

should be to accomplish "the praise of the glory of his grace" Ephesians 1:6, KJV.

LET THE HOLY SPIRIT GUIDE YOUR GROUP TO DEVELOP ITS OWN UNIQUE PERSONALITY!

INDEX

304

305

308

311

314

315